Essential
Scotland

by Hugh Taylor
& Moira McCrossan

*Above: the Trossachs. Wilderness of the outlaw
Rob Roy MacGregor*

AAA Publishing
1000 AAA Drive, Heathrow, Florida 32746

*Above: Scotch whisky –
the Water of Life in
miniature*

Front cover AA World
Travel Library/Ken
Paterson: *Cavalry
marching in the
Edinburgh Festival*
Back cover AA World
Travel Library/Jim Carnie:
Drumlanrig Castle

Written by Hugh Taylor & Moira McCrossan

Reprinted Feb 2005

Edited, designed and produced by AA Publishing
© Automobile Association Developments Limited 2004

OS Ordnance Survey® This product includes mapping data
licensed from Ordnance Survey® with
the permission of the Controller of Her Majesty's
Stationery Office. © Crown copyright 2005. All rights
reserved. Licence number 399221.

Mapping produced by the Cartographic Department of The
Automobile Association

Library of Congress Catalog Card Number: on file

ISBN 1–56251–588–8

Published in the United States by AAA Publishing,
1000 AAA Drive,
Heathrow, Florida 32746
Published in the United Kingdom By AA Publishing

A02556

Colour separation: Chroma Graphics (Overseas) Pte Ltd,
Singapore

Printed and bound in Italy by Printer Trento S.r.l.

Find out more about
AAA Publishing and the
wide range of services
the AAA provides by
visiting our website at
www.aaa.com

The weather chart on **page 118** of this book is
calibrated in °C. For conversion to °F simply use the
following formula:

$$°F = 1.8 \times °C + 32$$

Contents

About this Book 4

Viewing Scotland 5–14

The Authors' Scotland	6
Scotland's Features	7
Essence of Scotland	8–9
The Shaping of Scotland	10–11
Peace and Quiet	12–13
Scotland's Famous	14

Top Ten 15–26

Burns National Heritage Park	16
Burrell Collection	17
Culloden Battlefield	18
Edinburgh Castle	19
Glen Coe	20–21
New Lanark	22
Rosslyn Chapel	23
Skara Brae	24
The Tenement House, Glasgow	25
Traquair House	26

What to See 27–90

Edinburgh and the Borders	30–43
In the Know	38–39
Glasgow and the Southwest	44–59
Food and Drink	60–61
Central Scotland	62–73
The North	74–90

Where To... 91–116

Eat and Drink	92–99
Stay	100–105
Shop	106–109
Take the Children	110–11
Be Entertained	112–16

Practical Matters 117–24

Index 125–26

Acknowledgements 126

About this Book

KEY TO SYMBOLS

✚ map reference to the maps found in the What to See section

✉ address or location

☎ telephone number

◷ opening times

🍴 restaurant or café on premises or near by

Ⓢ nearest underground train station

🚌 nearest bus/tram route

🚆 nearest overground train station

🛳 ferry crossings and boat excursions

🛈 tourist information

♿ facilities for visitors with disabilities

✋ admission charge

↔ other places of interest near by

❓ other practical information

➤ indicates the page where you will find a fuller description

✈ travel by air

This book is divided into five sections to cover the most important aspects of your visit to Scotland.

Viewing Scotland pages 5–14
An introduction to Scotland by the authors.
Scotland's Features
Essence of Scotland
The Shaping of Scotland
Peace and Quiet
Scotland's Famous

Top Ten pages 15–26
The authors' choice of the Top Ten places to see in Scotland, listed in alphabetical order, each with practical information.

What to See pages 27–90
The four main areas of Scotland, each with its own brief introduction and an alphabetical listing of the main attractions.
Practical information
Snippets of 'Did you know…' information
3 suggested walks
4 suggested tours
2 features

Where To… pages 91–116
Detailed listings of the best places to eat, stay, shop, take the children and be entertained.

Practical Matters pages 117–24
A highly visual section containing essential travel information.

Maps
All map references are to the individual maps found in the What to See section of this guide.
For example, Edinburgh Castle has the reference ✚ 34C2 – indicating the page on which the map is located and the grid square in which the castle is to be found. A list of the maps that have been used in this travel guide can be found in the index.

Prices
Where appropriate, an indication of the cost of an establishment is given by **£** signs:
£££ denotes higher prices, **££** denotes average prices, while **£** denotes lower charges.

Star Ratings
Most of the places described in this book have been given a separate rating:

✪✪✪ Do not miss
✪✪ Highly recommended
✪ Worth seeing

Viewing
Scotland

The Authors' Scotland   6
Scotland's Features   7
Essence of Scotland   8–9
The Shaping of Scotland
       10–11
Peace and Quiet   12–13
Scotland's Famous   14

Above: *Eilean Donan, Scotland's most
romantic castle*
Right: *Kirkcudbright's ancient market place
was marked by this 17th-century Celtic cross*

5

The Authors' Scotland

Celtic Music

Celtic music is flavour of the moment and comprises the music of the seven Celtic Countries – Scotland, Ireland, Wales, the Isle of Man, Cornwall, Brittany and Galicia – all bound by a common thread but each unique and individual. Essentially a living tradition, it is currently undergoing a renaissance with young musicians experimenting and blending it with jazz and rock. To sample it at its best, head to one of the many pub sessions.

Above: *few sights and sounds can compare with a marching pipe band at Highland Games*
Below: *Goat Fell on the isle of Arran provides the ideal line for a shot to the green*

Some visitors to Scotland are looking for their roots and the ancestors who left these shores centuries earlier. Others come for the scenery, food, golf and culture. To each, however, Scotland is different, and that about sums it up, for trying to describe Scotland is a bit like trying to describe the wind. Just when you think you've got it, it changes direction.

The central belt, industrialised and scarred yet displaying an awesome beauty, includes the two great cities of Edinburgh and Glasgow, contrasting and yet complementing each other. The rolling hills and lush pastures of the South evoke emotions of a time long past, while in the Highlands there's a sense of wilderness created by the towering mountain ranges, dark, mysterious lochs and long, lonely glens.

Scotland is also a land of history where the past is very close. Castles, fortified towers and battlefields from warfaring ages sit beside prehistoric stone monuments the equal of any in Europe.

Then there are the people – independent, argumentative, philosophical – descended from the Celts, integrating successive waves of Italian, Asian and Polish immigrants along the way. We are the Scots and we take great delight in introducing visitors to our food, culture, history, music, sport and politics. Talk to us, join us in song and dance while we celebrate everything and anything in the pubs, bars and at ceilidhs (► 38). But take care, you might never want to go home.

Scotland's Features

Geography

The popular image of Scotland is of heather-clad mountains, rivers, islands and lochs. The total land area is 77,080sq km (30,405 square miles), much of it sparsely populated islands and mountainous areas. Scotland has around 800 islands, of which about 130 are inhabited. Because of the number of islands and the numerous long sea lochs and estuaries, the 10,000-km (6,215-mile) coastline is vast in relation to the size of the country. The Cairngorms in the north of Scotland is the largest area of peaks over 1,000m in the UK and includes the highest mountain, Ben Nevis, at 1,344m. There are about 30,000 lochs and 50,000km (30,000 miles) of river, which are among the least polluted in the world.

Climate

The north of Shetland, on the same latitude as the south of Greenland, is closer to the Arctic circle than to London, however, the climate of Scotland in general is temperate but changeable. The Gulf Stream, which bathes the west coast in a warm flow of water from the Gulf of Mexico, moderates temperatures in the west, while rain blows in from the Atlantic. The east tends to be cooler and drier. In the Highlands, snow is common in winter, often closing roads completely.

Population

The population of Scotland is 5,136,000, most of which is concentrated in the central belt, the broad lowland area between Glasgow and Edinburgh. Scotland is one of the least densely populated areas of Europe – around 66 persons per sq km.

Spectacular view over the snow-scattered Cairngorms from Cairngorm summit

Politics and Society
Scotland is divided into 32 local authorities ranging in size from tiny Clackmannanshire to the City of Glasgow. In 1999, Scotland elected the first Scottish parliament for 300 years, taking over responsibility for all domestic matters from education and health to roads and transportation. Areas such as foreign policy and social security remain within the jurisdiction of the UK parliament.

Essence of Scotland

Horridge

Horridge – a combination of horrid and porridge – is a collection of poems by the Dumfriesshire poet Hugh McMillan, taking a satirical swipe at Scottish kitsch from tartan to shortbread tins and tea towels.
*'Here's tae us
Wha's like us
Damn few
And they're a' on teatowels.'*

Queen Victoria's favourite view of Loch Tummel

When Bonnie Prince Charlie fled from Culloden in 1746, he left behind the recipe for Drambuie, a famous whisky-based liqueur, and a legend that launched a thousand biscuit tins. The legislation banning kilt and tartan was ultimately repealed and they were popularised by Walter Scott, and later by Queen Victoria's love affair with the Highlands. The kitsch and sentimental nonsense spawned from these times bore little resemblance to the real Scotland, but with the passage of time it has been absorbed and is now as much a part of the essence of the country as the lochs and mountains, literature, arts, science, engineering and inventions.

THE **10** ESSENTIALS

If you only have a short time to visit Scotland, or would like to get a really complete picture of the country, here are the essentials:

• **Sample malt whisky.** There are so many varieties to choose from, but try the peaty taste of Islay Bowmore and the smooth, almost velvet quality of Grants Balvenie.

• **Drive the coast road from Ayr to Girvan.** Look out to Arran, Kintyre, the craggy rock of Ailsa Craig and, on a clear day, the coastline of Ireland.

• **Ride the train from Inverness to Kyle of Lochalsh.** This is one of the most scenic rail routes in Britain, particularly from the special observation cars.

• **Go to a pub music session.** The finest traditional Scottish music is found in informal pub sessions. Try the Scotia Bar in Glasgow (► 113).

• **Eat haggis, neeps and tatties.** Scotland's national dish is on the menu in many pubs and restaurants. Wash it down with a wee dram of whisky.

• **Go to a village gala.** Most small villages have a gala day with street parades, crowning of the Gala Queen, outdoor activities and a ceilidh in the village hall.

• **Visit one of the great abbey ruins in the South.** Even in ruins these are awesome. See Jedburgh and Melrose in the Borders or Dundrennan and Sweetheart in Dumfries and Galloway.

• **Visit the Museum of Scotland.** Opened in January 1999, this tells Scotland's story from the geological creation of the land to 20th-century industry.

• **Visit Glasgow's Barras.** Listen to the patter of the vendors at this famous flea market in the east end.

• **Visit Edinburgh Castle.** If you see only one thing, it has to be this. Then walk down the historic Royal Mile to the Palace of Holyroodhouse and the new Scottish Parliament.

Magnificent red sandstone remains of the Cistercian Abbey of Melrose

What could be better than a taste of haggis washed down with a wee dram?

The Shaping of Scotland

2000 BC
Early Pictish peoples settle the land and live by farming, hunting and fishing.

AD 80–142
The Romans make Hadrian's Wall the final frontier of the Roman Empire.

9th–12th century
Kenneth MacAlpin (c 843–58) and Duncan I (1034–40) are among the first kings of Scotland, while David I (1124–53) organises the state and the establishment of the great abbeys.

1292–1314
The Scottish Wars of Independence
John Balliol becomes king with the support of Edward I of England in 1292. When he allies with France, Edward crushes him at Dunbar. William Wallace wages a guerilla campaign, leading the Scots to victory at the Battle of Stirling Bridge (1297), only to be defeated at the Battle of Falkirk (1298). He is finally betrayed in 1305 and executed in London. Robert Bruce is crowned king in 1307 and defeats the English at Bannockburn in 1314.

1544–5
'The Rough Wooing'
Henry VIII tries to force the betrothal of his infant son to the infant Mary, Queen of Scots, by a series of border raids. This drives the Scots back towards the Auld Alliance with France.

Wallace's historic defeat of the English at Stirling Bridge in 1297

Mary is betrothed to the Dauphin and sent to France in 1548. In 1560, the Reformation is declared and papal authority renounced. Mary returns to Scotland after the death of her husband, clashes with John Knox, the Protestant reformer, and is implicated in the death of her husband, Lord Darnley. When she finally flees to England, she is imprisoned by Elizabeth I and executed in 1587.

1603
Mary's son, James VI, already King of Scotland, succeeds Elizabeth to the English throne. The Stuart dynasty is divided

Mary, Queen of Scots

by religious differences under Charles I and Charles II. The throne is offered to William of Orange in 1690.

1707
Tensions between the parliaments of Scotland and England lead to the Union of Parliaments, effectively abolishing the Scottish parliament.

1715 and 1745
Support for the cause of the Stuart claimant James VII of Scotland (James II of England) leads to Jacobite risings. The first, in 1715, is fuelled by the accession of George I and resentments against the Union, while the second, in 1745, is led by Bonnie Prince Charlie, who is defeated at Culloden in 1746.

Early 19th century
The landowners in the Highlands evict families and raze their houses to make way for profitable sheep. The Highlands are emptied of people, some to the newly industrial lowlands, while others emigrate to the New World.

20th century
Government becomes more democratic and suffrage is extended to women. The rise of the trade union movement, together with rent strikes and the socialist campaigner John MacLean, gain Glasgow the reputation as Red Clydeside. The founding of the Scottish Nationalist Party in 1928 indicates a resurgence in the desire for self determination which has ebbed and flowed over the century. After the referendum for a Scottish Parliament in 1998, Donald Dewar, the Scottish Secretary declares, 'There shall be a Scottish Parliament – I like that.'

1 July 1999
The Scottish Parliament reopens after nearly 300 years.

The new Scottish Parliament's temporary home on Edinburgh's Mound

Peace & Quiet

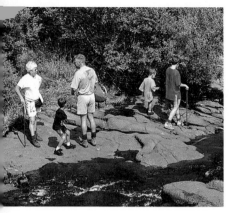

There are many sparsely populated areas of Scotland where the tranquillity seeps into you. You can walk through forests and over moors and mountains without seeing a single other person and on the top of some of the hills you could truly believe you were the last person on earth. On uninhabited islands, in the wild flow country (ancient peat bogs) of the north or in the pastoral landscapes in the Borders, it is easy to enjoy the solitude.

Family walking on a rocky trail by a burbling burn in Arran

Water

Scotland is surrounded by sea, and on remote Shetland or the Mull of Galloway you can find long stretches of isolated beaches or rocky coves with not a soul in sight. Although Dundee is a busy town, just a few miles away you will find the sandy beach of Broughty Ferry. There are always people there, walking their dogs, picking up shells or driftwood or gazing out over the broad calm waters of the Tay, but it's an agreeable companionship as you smile and pass by. In many cities, and across the industrial heartlands, there are the historic byways of old canals such as the Union Canal in Edinburgh, now converted to leisure activities, where you can walk or cycle on the towpath or take a slow boat to nowhere along a tree-lined corridor behind the city streets. In the hills, moorlands and mountains of Scotland you can always hear the sound of rushing burns, tumbling over stones down rocky steps, or, hidden at the foot of a glen, a river winding gently down into some still reflective loch.

Parks and Forests

In countryside or city, you are never far from pleasant parkland or forest trails. Glasgow, known as the 'Dear Green Place' because of its extensive parks, has Glasgow Green at its very heart. Edinburgh is a city full of gardens. At the bottom of the Royal Mile, through Dunbar Close, there is a secret little 17th-century garden, with herb gardens and stone seats, where you can escape from the hurly-burly to a tiny green haven. There are vast areas of forest everywhere in Scotland, many of them with way-marked forest trails. There can be nothing more calming than walking through miles of forest, suddenly emerging at the top of a hill with a glorious view or finding ancient bridges or Celtic crosses by the wayside. There are several way-marked forest walks around the lovely village of Dunkeld in Perthshire; you can walk by the rivers and find the old Birnam oak, a sole survivor of the ancient Caledonian forest or the 65m Douglas fir and enormous cedar of Lebanon on the Hermitage woodland walk.

Above: *the clifftop path from Portpatrick to Dunskey Castle*
Below: *the Hermitage Bridge near Dunkeld*

Churches

In Dunkeld you can visit Dunkeld Cathedral, and there are many churches, abbeys and sacred places all over the country in which you can find solace and a quiet retreat. From the great Border abbeys and the lovely medieval gem of Rosslyn Chapel to the perfect little Italian chapel created by the POWs in Orkney and the standing stones of Callanish, there are places of ritual and prayer for quiet and reflective contemplation.

Scotland's Famous

Robert Burns

One of the world's greatest poets was born in Alloway, near Ayr, in 1759. Robert Burns was greatly influenced by the singing and story-telling of his mother, Agnes Broun. He became a celebrity after the publication of his first volume of poems, *The Kilmarnock Edition*, was feted by Edinburgh society, and travelled throughout Scotland. After an unsuccessful farming venture at Ellisland in Dumfriesshire, he obtained a commission as an Excise man in Dumfries where he continued until his untimely death in 1796. Single-handed, he rescued and preserved the core of the Scottish song tradition through his work on Johnstone's Scots Musical Museum.

Robert Burns, Scotland's Bard

Auld Lang Syne
Academics argue that the hand of Burns is evident in *Auld Lang Syne*. He *did* rework many old songs, but he never claimed it of this one. Burns described it as 'the old Song of the olden times, which has never been in print, nor even in manuscript, untill I took it down from an old man's singing.'

Mary, Queen of Scots

Mary is one of Scotland's most romantic characters. Queen of Scots from the age of six, she was betrothed to the Dauphin of France, and raised as a Frenchwoman. Following the Dauphin's death she returned to rule Scotland in 1561. At 18, effectively a foreigner in her own country, Mary clung to her Catholic religion, incurring the wrath of the misogynist Protestant reformer John Knox. Her reign was short and tragic, clouded by intrigue, suspicion and murder. Eventually defeated, she fled to England where, after a long imprisonment, she was beheaded at Fotheringay in 1587.

William Wallace

Wallace, a shadowy historical figure, was born at Ellerslie in Ayrshire. He won a remarkable victory against a vastly superior English force at the Battle of Stirling Bridge in 1297. Created Guardian of Scotland, he recaptured Berwick but was eventually betrayed by the perfidious Scottish nobility. He was hung, drawn and quartered at Tyburn, London, in 1305.

Sir Sean Connery

Sean Thomas Connery was born in Edinburgh in 1930. His big break came in 1962 when he was cast as Secret Agent James Bond. He won an Oscar in 1987 and was later voted the World's Sexiest Man. Connery is a passionate supporter of the Scottish National Party.

Top Ten

Burns National Heritage Park 16
Burrell Collection 17
Culloden Battlefield 18
Edinburgh Castle 19
Glen Coe 20–21
New Lanark 22
Rosslyn Chapel 23
Skara Brae 24
The Tenement House,
   Glasgow 25
Traquair House 26

Above: *medieval stained glass from Sir
William Burrell's amazing art collection*
Right: *a Scottish piper, a sight often
seen on the streets of Edinburgh*

1

Burns National Heritage Park

Alloway was Robert Burns' birthplace and the setting for his well-loved poem of ghosts and witches Tam o' Shanter.

✚ 54B3

✉ Alloway

☎ 01292 443700

🕓 Apr–Oct, daily 9:30–5:30 (10–5 in wnter)

🍴 Restaurant (£)

🚌 Hourly bus Ayr to Alloway. Western 57

🚆 Nearest train station Ayr

♿ Very good

✋ Moderate

↔ Culzean Castle and Country Park (▶ 53)

View of the Burns Monument and River Doon from the bridge where Tam o' Shanter escaped the witches

Robert Burns' father, William Burnes, built his 'auld clay biggin' near the banks of the River Doon, with walls 1m thick and tiny windows to protect against the chill Scottish winters. This long, low, thatched cottage, where Robert was born, still stands today, restored to its original condition, at the centre of the Burns National Heritage Park. Among the fascinating memorabilia on display are a plaster cast of the poet's skull, his Bible, and various original manuscripts, including the world's most famous song of parting *Auld Lang Syne*.

The manuscript of *Tam o' Shanter*, also on view in the cottage, is translated into virtual reality at the nearby visitors' centre in the Tam o' Shanter Experience. This hilarious and atmospheric tale recounts how the hapless Tam, in a drunken stupor, blunders upon the witches, then entranced by the pretty young Nannie, roars out, 'Weel done Cutty sark!', only to be chased from Alloway Kirk to the Brig o' Doon by a 'hellish legion' of witches. The reality of 'Alloway's auld haunted kirk' is close by and in this eerie ruin it is easy to imagine the open coffins and malignant tokens of the poem. Follow the chase from here to the Brig o' Doon, where Tam's mare Meg lost her tail to the winsome witch. This narrow old stone bridge was on the main road from Ayr to Carrick, a route well trodden by Burns, and gives some idea of the primitive state of Scotland's roads 200 years ago.

2
Burrell Collection

This wonderful museum is built around an exquisite, idiosyncratic collection, gathered over a period of 80 years.

The Rehearsal, *by Degas, from the Burrell Collection*

The millionaire shipping magnate Sir William Burrell left his eclectic collection of paintings, tapestries, stained glass, furniture, silver and precious objects of all kinds to the people of Glasgow in 1944. He was a magpie who started collecting as a boy and continued until his death in 1958, by which time his acquisitions numbered some 8,000 treasures and artefacts from around the world.

For years the collection lay in dusty storerooms until the present building in Pollok Country Park was constructed in 1983 to house it, enhancing it and adorned by it. This red sandstone, wood and glass structure nestles in a corner of the parkland next to a grove of chestnut and sycamore. Inside, the great glass walls bring the woodlands into the heart of the museum. Medieval stone doorways and windows have been built into the fabric of the building, antique stained glass hangs before the glass walls and the rooms are clad in ancient tapestries. Three rooms from Burrell's home at Hutton Castle have been re-created with their windows looking out on to the glass-roofed central courtyard. The collection is particularly strong on rare oriental porcelain and fine medieval French tapestries, but includes paintings by Cezanne and Degas and sculptures by Rodin. It is intriguing not just for the objects and the building but because of the man who assembled it.

➕ 46A1

✉ Pollok Country Park, Glasgow

☎ 0141 287 2550

🕐 Mon–Thu and Sat, 10–5, Fri and Sun 11–5

🍴 Restaurant (££)

🚌 45, 48A and 57 from the centre of Glasgow

🚆 Pollokshaws West

♿ Very good

✋ Free

17

3
Culloden Battlefield

✚ 79D3

✉ 10km (6 miles) east of Inverness

☎ 01463 790607

🕐 Moor always open. Visitors' centre daily Apr–Jun and Sep–Oct, 9–6; Jul–Aug 9–7; Feb–Mar and Nov–Dec 11–4. Closed Christmas and Jan

🚌 Highland Country Buses from Inverness

♿ Good

✋ Cheap

↔ Fort George (▶ 81)

Old Leanach Cottage, as it was on 16 April, 1746, at the Battle of Culloden

This desolate moor, where the last battle on British soil was fought, was the scene of savage slaughter after the defeat of the Jacobites.

This bleak moorland has been restored to the condition it was in on that fateful morning in 1746 when the hopes of the Royal House of Stuart to regain the throne of Scotland were forever dashed. It is a melancholy site where, tradition has it, the birds never sing and where no heather grows on the graves of the clansmen slaughtered in the aftermath by the forces of the Duke of Cumberland.

The broad, windswept expanse of Culloden Moor was ideal for the government's cavalry and artillery – the entrenched guns laid waste the Highland ranks. When finally the Highlanders charged, they became bogged down in the mud and scattered in disorder. Their infantry, already outnumbered, exhausted and starving after the long march from Derby, faltered and fell under a murderous hail of shot. The wounded survivors were slaughtered where they lay, and indiscriminate butchery of men, women and children was encouraged by Cumberland on the road to Inverness. The following year, all weapons, bagpipes, tartan and the kilt were banned by law in a bid to destroy the Highland culture and the clan system. Today, the episode is described in an excellent audio-visual in the visitor centre.

The Battle of Culloden was the last battle of the Jacobite rebellion of 1745, and the final defeat was followed by savage cruelty and years of persecution. An oppressive sadness and poignancy surrounds the memorial cairns, the sort of atmosphere that clings to such places as the Somme and Auschwitz which have witnessed pitiless waste of human life.

4
Edinburgh Castle

Home to monarchs, scene of banquets and siege, this castle is not only at the heart of Scotland's capital but of its history.

Edinburgh Castle dominates the city from every angle and is visible from miles away. Over a million people visit every year and the queues for the Crown Room start to form early every day. The ancient Honours of Scotland are the oldest crown jewels in Europe, and the Stone of Destiny on which all Scots monarchs were crowned is also on view here.

There's been a fortification on this great volcanic rock since Celtic times, and the tiny Norman St Margaret's Chapel, the oldest building in Edinburgh, has stood intact for more than 900 years. The newly restored Royal Apartments include the room where Mary, Queen of Scots gave birth to the future James VI of Scotland (James I of England). The Great Hall has seen many historic gatherings and is still used for receptions by the Scottish First Minister. In the castle's cellar is the colossal cannon called Mons Meg, which fired its massive stone cannon-balls at the Battle of Flodden in 1513, a devastating defeat for the Scots by the English. At 1PM you can witness the firing of the one o'clock gun – not Mons Meg! The custom, which dates back to an era when few people owned clocks or watches, distinguishes the residents from the visitors. Visitors are often startled, Edinburgh folk just check their watches.

In August, the Castle Esplanade is the venue for the world-famous Edinburgh Military Tattoo. For three weeks the Army presents a dramatic, floodlit programme of music, marching and historical re-enactments. Almost as impressive as the castle itself are the views of the city of Edinburgh and surrounding countryside from its ramparts.

➕ 34C2

✉ At the top of the Royal Mile

☎ 0131 225 9846

🕐 Apr–Oct, daily 9:30–6 (5 in winter)

🚆 Waverley

♿ Poor

✋ Expensive

↔ Grassmarket and Museum of Scotland (▶ 32), Palace of Holyroodhouse and People's Story (▶ 33), Princes Street Gardens and the Scottish Parliament (▶ 36)

Edinburgh Castle, spectacularly set atop its volcanic crag

19

5
Glen Coe

 78C2

✉ 24km (15 miles) south of Fort William

🍴 Snack bar in Glencoe Village (£)

🚌 Highland Country Buses from Fort William; Scottish City Link from Glasgow and Fort William

Buachaille Etive Beag, the Small Shepherd of Etive, looks down on Lochan na Fol, Glen Coe

This majestic mountain pass running from Glencoe village to Rannoch Moor is one of the most spectacular and desolate sights in Scotland.

Lying at the foot of massive mountains, often disappearing into heavy swirling cloud, the gloom in Glen Coe can be oppressive. Under clear blue skies, the smooth green humps of the mountains, the rocky summits of the Three Sisters, the wide floor of the glen and the distant mountain tops beyond are a familiar sight the world over on calendars and in films. *Braveheart*, *Restless Natives*, *Highlander* and many other movies were shot in the Glen.

There is an awesome stillness about the Glen, which even the great numbers of tourists, walkers and climbers never disturb. However, its peace was rudely shattered on a winter morning over 300 years ago when Glen Coe became a byword for treachery. The chief of the Clan

MacDonald was late in swearing allegiance to the Crown. Campbell of Glenlyon, under orders signed by King William, took his men to Glencoe to make an example of the MacDonalds. He billeted his men there on the pretext that they were just passing through. In the early dawn of 13 February, 1692, throughout the glen, the Campbells dragged MacDonald men from their beds and murdered them, burning the houses as they went. The women, some carrying infants, fled into the mountains in a piercing snow storm, many perishing miserably.

Nowadays the unpredictable weather still claims lives among the skiers, walkers and climbers who flock to the Glen. There are countless challenging walks and climbs, but this is no land for a casual afternoon stroll.

In summer a trip up the ski lift to the summit will be rewarded by spectacular views over Rannoch Moor and the surrounding mountains.

Above: the steep snow-covered slopes of Glen Coe are very popular with skiers

6
New Lanark

54C4

In a gorge below Lanark

01555 661345

Daily 11–5

Tea room (£)

Bus service from station in Lanark

Lanark

Horsemarket, Ladyacre Road, Lanark ☎ 01555 661661

Good

Moderate

New Lanark was the first example of a working environment planned to consider the welfare of the workforce as well as efficiency and profit.

This was Robert Owen's utopian village, built near the Falls of Clyde to harness the power of the water for driving the cotton mills. New Lanark was much more than a mill town, it was a model village and Owen (1771–1858) was the forerunner of the great Victorian philanthropists who built towns such as Saltaire and Port Sunlight. Contrary to the wisdom of the time, Owen believed that a happy workforce would be a productive workforce, so he provided modern housing, a shop, a school and recreation facilities. His employees also worked shorter hours and had better working conditions, schooling was compulsory and he did not employ children under 10 in the mill.

His competitors thought he was crazy and that his business would suffer. They were astonished when it became more profitable rather than less. New Lanark survived as a mill town into the 20th century and was saved from ultimate demolition when it was restored as a conservation project. You can tour the houses, gardens and recreation hall, see the restored looms working and learn about life at the time through the eyes of a young girl in the Annie McLeod Experience.

Although it is in the industrial heartland of Scotland, New Lanark is set in a rural location on the banks of the Clyde. This was part of Owen's plan that his workers should live in pleasant surroundings. You can follow the delightful riverside walk to the Falls of Clyde to appreciate the importance of this.

Robert Owen built his New Lanark spinning mills on the banks of the River Clyde

7
Rosslyn Chapel

This tiny, atmospheric, medieval chapel is an exquisite masterpiece of the mason's art, with an unrivalled range and delicacy of carving.

Rosslyn Chapel with the famed Apprentice Pillar on the left

Rosslyn Chapel is possibly the most mysterious building in Scotland, like a great medieval cathedral in miniature. It is richly carved, including the most complete *danse macabre* (dance of death) in Europe and, if you know where to look, you will see the death mask of King Robert the Bruce, reproduced in stone. Built by Sir William St Clair, it has strong connections with the Knights Templar, a mystical order of wealthy warrior monks, who fought with Robert the Bruce at Bannockburn (1314). They were credited with finding the Holy Grail and the treasures of Solomon.

It is said that the Holy Grail is hidden in the Apprentice Pillar, one of two great pillars. The story goes that the apprentice saw the pillar in a dream and carved it in his master's absence. The master was so angry and jealous when he saw the delicate and complicated work that he felled the apprentice with a single blow of his mallet. The master was hanged, and his effigy and that of the apprentice and his mother can be found close to the pillars. Whatever the truth of the legends, there is no doubt that the master masons who chiselled these intricate patterns and medieval likenesses from stone were exceptionally gifted.

Whether it is the medieval faces peering out of the stone on all sides or the 20 knights in full armour interred below, there is an eerie supernatural feel to this tiny chapel and a strange chill as you enter the crypt. A former curator once saw the apparition of a monk kneeling before the altar with four spectral knights standing guard over him.

✚ 55D4

✉ Off Chapel Loan, opposite The Roslin Glen Hotel, Roslin (11.6km/7 miles south of Edinburgh)

☎ 0131 440 2159

🕐 Mon–Sat 10–5, Sun noon–4:45

🍴 Coffee shop (£)

🚌 315 from Edinburgh (First Lowland)

✋ Moderate

23

8
Skara Brae

 29C4

✉ 13km (8 miles) north of Stromness, Orkney

☎ 01856 841815

🕓 Mon–Sun 9:30–6:30, Apr–Oct; Mon–Sat 9:30–4:30, Sun 2–4:30, winter

✋ Moderate

An early dwelling at Skara Brae Stone Age settlement on Orkney

On a beautiful sandy sea-shore on the edge of the world is the perfectly preserved neolithic settlement of Skara Brae in Orkney.

Buried for centuries under the sand dunes of the Bay of Skail, a great storm in 1850 uncovered this complete Stone Age village which has been extensively excavated.

The villagers dug holes into the sandy soil so that their homes were half underground affording some protection against the winds. Interconnecting passages between the huts were lined with sandstone slabs. Wandering around the site and looking down into these homes is a poignant experience. The layout of the rooms resembles any small peasant dwelling – except that everything is made of stone. The dresser is a couple of flagstone shelves resting on stone 'legs', the bed is three slabs of stone set against the wall to form a 'box', and there is a central hearth.

There are few trees on Orkney, which is why these ancient people had to use alternative materials. Whale jawbones were probably used as rafters to support the roof, tools (displayed in the visitors' centre) were made of bone and stone, and pottery was richly decorated. They were farmers who bred cows and sheep and grew cereals, they walked on this ground, and looking into their homes, their lives seem vivid and close. An excellent reconstruction of one of the stone houses, complete with roof, is well worth a visit.

9
The Tenement House, Glasgow

Most of the population of industrial Scotland in the 19th and early 20th centuries lived in four- or five-storey tenement buildings similar to this one.

Miss Agnes Toward moved into this three-roomed flat with her mother in 1911 and lived there until her death in 1965. Houses in tenements ranged from the single end, which would nowadays be called a studio flat, to apartments such as this one, with several bedrooms and even a bathroom. Most flats had no inside toilet but several families would share one toilet off the stairs. Better classes of tenement building were distinguished by the 'wally close', with ornate patterned ceramic tiles on the walls of the entry.

The kitchen of a tenement flat, with the cooking range for warmth, was the centre of family life. Miss Toward's kitchen utensils lie on the deal (fir or pine) table, her jars of home-made jam are still sealed above, the washboard is in the deep ceramic sink and the washing hangs to dry on the pulley. The bed, built into the recess in the kitchen, consists of a lumpy mattress on boards and snow-white bed linen, and there is a another bed tucked away below to accommodate the large families which were the norm.

When Miss Toward died it was discovered that she had never thrown anything away. She had kept bus tickets, letters booking her holidays, even newspapers, which were piled high on chairs and tables. It was a treasure trove of ephemera, portraying a way of life that was passing, a tiny fragment of history caught in amber, and nostalgia for those who can remember it.

➕ 46B4

✉ 145 Buccleuch Street, Glasgow

☎ 0141 333 0183

🕐 Mar–Oct, daily 1–5 (last entry 4:30)

🚌 From Buchanan Street Bus Station

🚇 Charing Cross

✋ Moderate

↔ Glasgow School of Art (▶ 48)

Victorian middle-class parlour in Miss Toward's Tenement House

25

10
Traquair House

Dating from the early 12th century, Traquair claims to be the oldest continually inhabited house in Scotland.

✝ 55D3

✉ 2km (1½ miles) south of Innerleithen

☎ 01896 830323

🕐 Daily Jun–Aug, 10:30–5:30; Apr, May, Sep, 12–5; Oct, 11–4

🍴 Tea room (£)

🚌 62 from Edinburgh and Peebles to Innerleithen

✋ Expensive

The house was originally built as a hunting lodge for the Scottish kings and queens. Because of its strategic position on the banks of the River Tweed, it was fortified against border raids. James III gave it to his court musician, who sold it to the Earl of Buchan for £3 15s. Buchan's son James Stuart became the first laird, and from then on it developed as a family home. The main block was completed around 1600 and another two wings were added a century later. The famous Bear Gates were erected in 1737 at a cost of £12 15s for the pillars, £10 4s for the carving of the stone bears and four gallons of ale for the workmen. The gates opened into a long tree-lined avenue which Prince Charles Edward Stuart trod one late autumn day in 1745 as he set off on his ill-fated venture to try and reclaim the throne for the House of Stuart. The Earl swore that they would never be opened again until a Stuart returned to the throne of Scotland. To this day they remain sealed.

The extensive woodlands and gardens around Traquair are usually buzzing with activity – there are various craft workshops and a brewery. The beer is brewed in the old brew-house and fermented in the original 200-year-old oak casks. The maze next to the house is a delight for children of all ages, while the house itself is a labyrinth, with lots of quirky little steps and corridors and secret passages. Above all, it still has the feel of a family home.

Traquair House – a fine fortified Borders' castle

What to See

Edinburgh and the
   Borders   30–43
In the Know   38–9
Glasgow and the
   Southwest   44–59
Food and Drink   60–61
Central Scotland   62–73
The North   74–90

Above: *Balmoral was built for Queen Victoria in 1855*
Right: *a champion haggis-maker with his wares*

Orkney Islands

Fair Isle

Westray
Rousay
Sanday
Skara Brae
Stromness
Maes Howe
Stronsay
Kirkwall
Italian Chapel
Hoy
South Ronaldsay
Pentland Firth
Duncansby Head
Thurso
Wick

Shetland Islands

Yell
Unst
Fetlar
Hillswick
St Magnus Bay
Sandness
Whalsay
Foula
Scalloway
Bressay
Lerwick
Broch of Mousa
Jarlshof
Sumburgh Head

Fair Isle

Helmsdale
Dornoch Firth
Moray Firth
Elgin
Banff
Kinnaird Head
Fraserburgh
Nairn
Keith
Spey
Peterhead
Inverurie
Aviemore
Don
1309m
Mountains
Aberdeen
Braemar
Dee
Stonehaven
Pitlochry
Forfar
Montrose
Arbroath
Dundee
Tay
Firth of Tay
Perth
St Andrews
Kinross
Dunfermline
Firth of Forth
Falkirk
Kirkcaldy
Coatbridge
Dunbar
St Abb's Head
EDINBURGH
Eyemouth
Peebles
Galashiels
Tweed
Coldstream
Uplands
Jedburgh
Hawick
The Cheviot Hills

0   20   40   60   80   100 km
0   20   40   60 miles

Dumfries
Gretna Green
Firth

ENGLAND

C   D

29

Edinburgh & the Borders

Built on a series of volcanic rocks, Scotland's capital is undoubtedly one of the most beautiful cities of Europe. Few sights can compare with Princes Street Gardens laid out beneath the castle, massive on its dark crag of volcanic rock.

During the many wars with England, Edinburgh Castle was often the destination of the English armies and the area between the castle and the border was laid waste time and again. Even in times of peace, cross-border raids by cattle reivers (thieves) meant that the inhabitants of this region could never relax, but it was also an area of prosperity. Huge castles, built for defence, became grand dwellings of the aristocracy in times of peace. As you drive, cycle or walk through the rolling hills of the borders or along the rivers Yarrow, Tweed and Ettrick, the tranquillity belies its violent past.

> *'There's Gala Water,*
> *Leader Haughs, both lying*
> *right before us; and*
> *Dryburgh, where with*
> *chiming Tweed, the*
> *Lintwhites sing in chorus.'*

WILLIAM WORDSWORTH
1803

Top-notch social history museum in Edinburgh's Canongate Tolbooth

Edinburgh

Edinburgh is a city of two towns. Beside the castle are the narrow closes, winding streets and tall tenements of the Old Town, while opposite are the elegant classical squares, broad streets and peaceful gardens of the Georgian New Town. It's a joy to walk around this rich architectural tapestry, to stroll through gardens where suddenly the city bustle disappears into greenery and birdsong, or to climb the many hills and capture a glimpse of the Firth of Forth or majestic Arthur's Seat, and another perspective of this incomparable city.

What to See in Edinburgh

BRITANNIA ✪✪✪

Since the former royal yacht *Britannia* opened to the public at the Port of Leith in 1998, it has become Edinburgh's second-biggest attraction after the castle. There is an excellent visitors' centre with exhibits of photographs and reconstructed crews' cabins, but the real enticement is the yacht itself. You can peep into the Queen's bedroom, the royal sitting rooms and into various magnificently furnished state rooms which have witnessed momentous international receptions.

CALTON HILL ✪✪✪

Calton Hill is a superb vantage point from which to view the city, the Firth of Forth and the kingdom of Fife beyond. On Friday evenings you can also see the stars as the City Observatory is open to the public. The remainder of the buildings on Calton Hill are curious structures – the Nelson Monument is a telescope-shaped tower, while the uncompleted Greek temple is the National Monument to those killed in the Napoleonic Wars.

➕ 35E4

✉ Ocean Terminal, Leith
☎ 0131 555 8800
🕐 Daily 9:30–4:30
🍴 Excellent café on premises (£)
♿ Moderate
❓ Pre-booking recommended ☎ 0131 555 5566

➕ 35E4
🍴 Excellent restaurants near by (£–£££)

31

EDINBURGH CASTLE (► 19, TOP TEN)

GRASSMARKET   ✪✪✪

Edinburgh's first market area built outside the city walls has seen many changes over the years. From market-place to public execution site, it became a depressed slum area, frequented by down-and-outs. Recently, its fortunes have revived and it is now a cosmopolitan centre with an eclectic mix of shops and pubs. TV personality Clarissa Dickson Wright of *Two Fat Ladies* fame runs the Cook's Book Shop on the corner, while across the road, Stan Wood, Britain's only commercial palaeontologist, has his fossil shop. Along the brightly coloured façades in Victoria Street are a brush shop, a traditional cheesemonger, a French baker and an incredible indoor flea market called Byzantium.

MUSEUM OF SCOTLAND   ✪✪✪

Edinburgh's latest addition merges a bold modern design with the vaulted hall, cast-iron balconies and glass roof of the Royal Museum of Scotland to which is is adjoined. Displays are built into the walls, and by the tantalising use of arches and gaps, discrete spaces are created. Unlike the Royal Museum, which in true Victorian style has a wonderful miscellaneous selection of exhibits and curiosities ranging from across the globe, the new museum focuses on Scotland. The whole of Scotland's story, from prehistoric rocks and fossils to the late 20th century unfolds here. One of the more gruesome displays is the early Scottish guillotine, the Iron Maiden, along with the names of some of those who lost their heads to it. Among the exhibits in the display of 20th-century items representative of the century is a Fender Stratocaster guitar, chosen by the Prime Minister, Tony Blair.

34C2

⊪ Excellent cafés (£) and restaurants on the square

? Lot of nightlife, geared mainly to students and young people

---

35D2

✉ Chambers Street

☎ 0131 225 7534/247 4219

⏰ Mon–Sat 10–5 (Tue until 8), Sun noon–5

⊪ Excellent café (£) and high-class restaurant (£££) on premises

⛃ Free

The most colourful and eclectic collection of shops in Edinburgh is here in Victoria Street

PALACE OF HOLYROODHOUSE ✪✪

At the bottom of the spine of volcanic rock known as the Royal Mile sits Holyroodhouse Palace, home of Scottish monarchs since the 16th century, although most of the current building dates from 1671. It was here that Mary, Queen of Scots, spent much of her short, tragic reign, and

where she suffered the bigoted tirades of John Knox and witnessed the savage slaughter of her servant Riccio. Holyrood is the Queen's official residence in Scotland, but the state and historic apartments are open to the public.

Spreading out behind the palace, **Holyrood Park** is a wide open space dominated by the great volcanic plug known as Arthur's Seat. A climb to the top is rewarded with stunning views of Edinburgh, the kingdom of Fife and the Borders, and there are plenty of paths for less strenuous walking or cycling. Rock climbers and abseilers can practise their skills on Salisbury Crags, while the less energetic can just picnic by the pond. It is particularly peaceful on Sundays when cars are prohibited.

Edinburgh fishwife in wax at the People's Story museum

🏠 35F3
✉ Bottom of Royal Mile
☎ 0131 556 7371
🕐 Apr–Oct, Mon–Sat 9:30–5:15, Sun 10–4:30; Nov–Mar, daily 9:30–3:45 (closed Good Fri, early May, early Jun and late Jun to mid-Jul, or when the Queen is in residence; telephone to check)
🍴 Excellent tea room (£) just up Royal Mile
💷 Expensive

Holyrood Park
🕐 Open all hours
🍴 Excellent cafés/ restaurants on the Royal Mile (£)

THE PEOPLE'S STORY ✪✪

Situated in the former Canongate Tolbooth on the Royal Mile, this fascinating free museum of social history is one of the gems of Edinburgh. Re-creations of living quarters, workshops and displays of artefacts seek to explain the manner and quality of life for ordinary Edinburgh folk over the years.

🏠 35E3
✉ Canongate Tolbooth
☎ 0131 331 5545
🕐 Mon–Sat 10–5 (Sun 2–5 during Festival only)
🍴 Excellent café (£) across street 💷 Free

PRINCES STREET ✪✪✪

One of the great joys of shopping in Princes Street is the space. Only one side of the street has buildings, the other side is Princes Street Gardens (➤ 36), where you can escape the crowds. Jenner's, with its labyrinth of departments and tiers of polished balconies, is the world's oldest independent department store. If you tire of shopping, slip out the back door into Rose Street, which has more public houses than any other street in Scotland.

🏠 34B3
🍴 Excellent cafés/bars in Rose Street (£££)

34B3
 Snack bar in gardens (£)

*Princes Street Gardens
are a delight at all
seasons, but attract the
crowds on a warm
summer day*

PRINCES STREET GARDENS ✪✪✪

It is hard to believe that these carefully tended gardens
were once the Nor' Loch ('north loch'), into which ran all
the sewage of the Old Town. The gardens run the length
of Princes Street, divided into two parts by the Mound, the
pile of earth excavated when the New Town was built. The
Greek splendour of the Royal Scottish Academy and the
National Gallery of Scotland now occupy the site. Locals
and visitors alike relax in the gardens, enjoying the flowers,
admiring the famous Floral Clock, feeding the squirrels or
simply sitting in the shade of a willow tree or on one of the
polished wooden memorial benches. There's a bandstand
for summer concerts and an open-air café. On the last
night of the Festival, the spectacular Bank of Scotland
Fireworks Concert is staged here, and at New Year it hosts
the world's biggest Hogmanay (New Year's Eve) party.

 35F3
✉ Junction of Queen Street
and St Andrews Street
☎ 0131 556 8921
🕐 Mon–Sun 10–5 (closes
7 Thu)
🍴 Excellent café (£) on
premises
♿ Free

SCOTTISH NATIONAL PORTRAIT GALLERY ✪

In a Gothic red sandstone building on Queen Street, this
gallery offers a fascinating tour of the great and the good
of Scotland past and present. Among the kings and
queens in the collection are portraits of Mary, Queen of
Scots, as well as her persecutor John Knox and her ill-fated
husband Lord Darnley. Robert Burns, J M Barrie and Hugh
McDiarmid are among the literary greats, and living
subjects include the legendary accordionist Jimmy Shand.

 35F3
✉ George IV Bridge
☎ 0845 278 1999 (general
information)
🕐 Mon–Fri 9:30–5, Sat
Jul–Sep 9:30–5
🍴 Cafés and restaurants in
the Royal Mile (££)
♿ Free

THE SCOTTISH PARLIAMENT ✪✪

After a break of nearly 300 years, Scotland again has its
own Parliament. Since 1999 it has been in temporary
accommodation in the Church of Scotland Assembly at the
top of the Mound. Meanwhile, a futuristic new building is
being built at the bottom of the Royal Mile adjacent to the
Palace of Holyroodhouse and the Dynamic Earth exhibition
(► 110). The Parliament shop and visitors' centre are at
the corner of the Royal Mile and George IV Bridge.

Edinburgh Walk

This walk takes in the Old Town of Edinburgh, including the historic Grassmarket, the Royal Mile and Greyfriars Church. The view from Calton Hill at sunset is spectacular.

Begin on Castle Esplanade. At the end, turn down the steps to the Grassmarket. Cross Johnstone Terrace and continue to the bottom. Turn left along the Grassmarket.

Investigate the colourful shops of Victoria Street to the left and return to the Grassmarket.

Cross over into Candlemaker Row and go up to the statue of Greyfriars Bobby.

To the right is Greyfriars Church, where the faithful little terrier, Greyfriars Bobby, kept vigil over his master's grave, and opposite is the Museum of Scotland (➤ 32).

Turn left along George IV Bridge, then right down the Royal Mile.

You will pass St Giles Cathedral, the Museum of Childhood and John Knox's House. Have a look at the Palace of Holyroodhouse at the bottom (➤ 33).

Turn back up the Royal Mile to White Horse Close on the right. Go through it on to Calton Road. Turn left and take the steep steps on your right up to Regent Road. Cross and take the road leading up behind the Royal High School to Calton Hill.

On the way up you will find a cairn dedicated to the achievement of a Scottish Parliament. On Calton Hill pass the National Monument and Nelson's Monument (➤ 31).

Take the steps back to Regent Road. Turn right, cross the road and head towards Princes Street. After the Mound, enter Princes Street Gardens past the Floral Clock. Exit by the gate towards the castle and Ramsay Garden. Head up right through Ramsay Garden and return.

Distance
6km (4 miles)

Time
2–6 hours

Start/end point
Castle Esplanade
✚ 28C2

Lunch
Clarinda's Tea Room
☎ 0131 557 1888

Antonio David's portrait of Bonnie Prince Charlie, part of the collection at the National Portrait Gallery

In the Know

If you only have a short time to visit Scotland and would like to get a real flavour of the country, here are some ideas:

 10

Ways to Be a Local

Ask for a pint and a hauf in a pub. You'll get a pint of beer and a dram of whisky – not a pint and a half of beer.

Listen to a piper or a pipe band. This outdoor instrument stirs the blood of all true Scots.

Visit a session of the Scottish Parliament. The visitor centre at the top of the Royal Mile offers information about the parliament. Free tickets are available to watch the proceedings.

Eat a fish supper or a smoked sausage supper while sitting on a harbour wall, watching the boats.

Drink Irn-Bru. This sweet orange-coloured drink is the classic hangover cure and typifies the worst in Scottish preferences.

Go for afternoon tea in a village or church hall. These fund-raising events offer delicious home baking.

Go for a sail 'doon the watter'. Take a trip on the *Waverley*, the world's last ocean-going paddle steamer, from Glasgow to the Clyde resorts.

Look for your name in the lists of clan tartans. Many people have a tartan even if they don't realise that their name is Scottish.

The silvery Tay has some of Scotland's best fishing

Read the *Sunday Post* which is full of sentimental stories and Scottish kitsch, and is sent to exiled Scots all over the world. The best bits are the comic strips of *Oor Wullie* and *The Broons*.

Go to a ceilidh at a hotel or a village hall or at one of the many folk music festivals which take place in the summer.

 10

Good Places to Have Lunch

The Ceilidh Place ✉ West Argyll Street, Ullapool ☎ 01854 612103. Fresh bread, hearty soups, a good vegetarian option and home baking.

The Garden Café ✉ Lennoxlove ☎ 01620 822156. The lovely setting of Lennoxlove House and gardens (➤ 40) and imaginative menu make it a relaxing lunch experience.

Henderson's ✉ 94 Hanover Street, Edinburgh ☎ 0131 225 2131. Well-known vegetarian salad bar with usually four or five hot choices, changing throughout the day, with puddings to die for.

Hullabaloo Restaurant ✉ Robert Burns Centre, Mill Road, Dumfries ☎ 01387 259679. Tasty, innovative food with a wonderful vegetarian selection. Very small and popular. Booking essential.

The Lemon Tree ✉ 5 West North Street, Aberdeen ☎ 01224 642230. BBC Scotland broadcasts live shows from here. Good soups, vegetarian options and substantial basic fare.

Monty's ✉ 5 Mounthooly Street, Lerwick ☎ 01595 696555. Sophisticated dining in the evening, simple high-quality dishes at lunch time.

Nardini's ✉ The Promenade, Largs ☎ 01475 674555. Enormous '50s-style seaside café. The décor is pure nostalgia and the ice-cream is legendary.

Tartan at MacNaughton's of Pitlochry

78, St Vincent Street ⊠ Glasgow ☎ 0141 248 7878. Imaginative, high-quality food. Fresh Scottish ingredients with continental flair and excellent service.
Togs Café ⊠ 9 Templehill, Troon ☎ 01292 312868. Intimate art deco-style café, modernised in the 1950s with neon and Vitrolite. A reminder of the days when teenagers hugged a frothy coffee all evening and listened to Tommy Steele. Standard café food – bacon butties, chips and knickerbocker glories.
Valvona and Crolla ⊠ Leith Walk, Edinburgh ☎ 0131 556 6066. A wonderful Italian delicatessen (fresh pestos, cheeses, olive oils, breads and wines) with a stylish café at the back.

Top Activities

Climbing. The Highlands is the main area for climbing, with Aviemore as the main centre; there are strenuous opportunities in the Southern Uplands.
Walking through hills, mountains, moorlands, forests, along way-marked long-distance footpaths (the West Highland Way, the Southern Upland Way), and marked walks in country parks and estates.

Fishing. For salmon and trout fishing get a day ticket from the appropriate private estate, angling club or local council. There is sea fishing at seaside resorts.
Golf is the national game. If you can't get on one of the championship courses try one of the municipal courses and private clubs that admit day visitors – Girvan, Ayrshire; Thornhill, Dumfriesshire; Strathaven, Lanarkshire; and the Gowf Club, Loudoun, near Galston, Ayrshire.
Curling, Scotland's other national game, is now an Olympic sport. Many towns and hotels have ice rinks and offer tuition. Dumfries Ice Bowl, the Magnum Leisure Centre, Irvine and the Aberdeen Beach Leisure Centre are a few.
Bird-watching. The many species which can be seen range from the ospreys at Grantown-on-Spey and puffins on Shetland to the Spitsbergen barnacle geese at Caerlaverock, Dumfries.
Cycling is a great way to tour Scotland. There has been a huge growth in cycle paths across the country and in many towns and cities, particularly Edinburgh.
Watersports. Sailing, canoeing, white-water rafting, water-skiing, swimming, windsurfing – you name it, Scotland has

it. Watersports centres include Loch Ken Watersports in Dumfriesshire, Raasay Outdoors Centre in Skye and Strathclyde Park.
Bowling attracts players of all ages. It's a summer pastime and many local clubs admit visitors.
Shooting. Thousands of acres of grouse moors are given over to this pastime. Clay pigeon shooting is much more fun and there are centres throughout Scotland.

Scottish Inventors

- John Logie Baird (television)
- Alexander Graham Bell (telephone)
- Sir James Simpson (anaesthetic)
- Charles Macintosh (waterproof coat)
- John Dunlop (pneumatic tyre)
- Kirkpatrick MacMillan (bicycle)
- John Loudon McAdam (tarmacadam)
- Robert Watson Watt (radar)
- James Dewar (vacuum flask)
- Alexander Fleming (penicillin)

Best Golf Courses

- St Andrews, Old Course
- Carnoustie
- Royal Troon
- Turnberry, Ailsa
- Turnberry, Arran
- Royal Dornoch
- Haggs Castle
- Old Prestwick
- Gullane
- Muirfield

What to See in the Borders

ABBOTSFORD HOUSE ✪✪

Sir Walter Scott (1771–1832) designed Abbotsford and lived there for the last 20 years of his life. The Scots Baronial design, with medieval towers and turrets, reflects his romantic side. The library, housing Scott's huge collection of rare books is light and airy and also displays his accumulation of bizarre Scottish memorabilia, from Bonnie Prince Charlie's hair to the crucifix carried by Mary, Queen of Scots, when she was beheaded.

HADDINGTON ✪✪

The historic town of Haddington, a mixture of broad tree-lined streets and medieval street plan, is an architectural delight. The High Street, with its lanes and closes and quaint shops, is fronted by the elegant Town House designed by William Adam. Near by is the classical frontage of Carlyle House. The childhood home of Jane Welsh Carlyle, wife of Thomas Carlyle, the Sage of Chelsea, is tucked away behind it. Around the corner lies Haddington House, the oldest house in town, complete with re-created 17th-century garden. Further on, the tranquil riverside walk leads to St Mary's Collegiate Church, steeped in historical significance. The marks of the bombardment by the English during the 'Rough Wooing'(► 10) are still visible. John Knox, the great Protestant reformer, preached here; the Lauderdale Aisle is an exquisite Episcopalian chapel; and two of the lovely stained-glass windows are by Sir Edward Burne-Jones.

Just beyond Haddington is **Lennoxlove**, set in 240ha of verdant woodlands. It appears to have grown in an endearing mixture of styles around a medieval tower and has a collection of furniture, paintings and mementoes of Mary, Queen of Scots, including her death mask.

✚ 55E3
✉ 3km (2 miles) west of Melrose
☎ 01896 752043
🕐 Mid-Mar to Oct, daily 9:30–5 (Mar–May and Oct, Sun 2–5)
🍴 Tea room on premises (£)
✋ Moderate

✚ 55E4

Lennoxlove
✉ 3km (2 miles) south of Haddington
☎ 01620 823720
🕐 Easter weekend–Oct, Wed, Thu and Sun 2–4:30 half hourly tours
🍴 Garden Café (£)
✋ Moderate

Haddington's Waterside Bistro is a popular spot for a summer lunch

JEDBURGH ✪✪✪

This lovely little town with its old wynds (alleys) and houses was established as a Royal Burgh in the 12th century. The immense, graceful ruin of Jedburgh Abbey, founded in 1138, gives the most complete impression of all the Border abbeys' great monastic institutions. It has a haunting abandoned feel to it, as if its medieval inhabitants might return next week to repair the roof. The mellow 16th-century tower house, known as Mary Queen of Scots' House, is worth a visit, too. It wasn't actually her house but she did stay here.

KELSO ✪

The small market town of Kelso has an enormous cobbled square with a cluster of Georgian houses around it and a maze of cobbled streets leading off. Kelso Abbey suffered badly during the 'Rough Wooing' (► 10), and not much remains. Floors Castle, a mile away along the Cobby Riverside walk, is a huge early 18th-century mansion designed by William Adam and still home to the Duke of Roxburgh.

Mellerstain House, a few miles distant, is possibly the finest Georgian mansion in Scotland, retaining the original Adam colours in its interior paintwork. Allow half a day to take in the superb collection of paintings, period furniture and terraced gardens.

MELROSE ✪

Nestling in the Eildon Hills, Melrose is yet another picturesque old abbey town. The heart of Robert the Bruce, who rebuilt the abbey, is buried here. Close by is a Roman three-hill fort, at Newstead, and the **Trimontium Exhibition** in Market Square tells that story.

> ### DID YOU KNOW?
>
> The word 'dunce' originated from the medieval academic John Duns Scotus who came from the Borders town of Duns. He taught in Oxford and Paris, but when his ideas went out of fashion anyone espousing them became known as a Duns.

✚ 55E3
✉ 16km (10 miles) southwest of Kelso
☎ 01835 863925
🕐 Apr–Sep, daily 9:30–6:30; Oct–Mar, Mon–Sat 9:30–4:30, Sun 2–4:30
🍴 Cafés and restaurants (£) near by in town
👐 Cheap
❓ Opening times also apply to Dryburgh and Melrose abbeys

✚ 55E3

Mellerstain House
✉ Gordon
☎ 01573 410225
🕐 Easter, May–Sep, Sun–Fri 12:30–5. Oct, Sat and Sun only
🍴 Restaurant (££)
👐 Moderate

Above: the majestic ruin of Jedburgh Abbey towers over the River Jed

✚ 55E3

Trimontium Exhibition
✉ Ormiston Institute, Market Square
☎ 01896 822651
🕐 Apr–Oct, daily 10:30–4:30. Closed 1–2 Sat and Sun
🍴 Cafés and restaurants (£) near by
👐 Cheap

41

55D3
✉ High Street, Innerleithen
☎ 01896 830206
🕙 Good Fri–Easter Mon and Jun–Sep Thu–Sat and Mon 12–5, Sun 1–5)
🍴 Cafés and restaurants (£) near by
✋ Cheap

55F4
🍴 Café (£) near harbour

At St Abbs Head the rolling hills of the Borders give way to rugged cliffs and the North Sea

ROBERT SMAILS PRINTING WORKS ✪✪

The pretty village of Innerleithen is where Robert Smail operated his High Street printing shop in the 19th century. Now in the care of the National Trust for Scotland, it is perfectly preserved. With its Victorian office, composing room, paper store and machine room, there are lots of working exhibits, some hands-on, which can produce authentic Victorian posters and handbills.

ROSSLYN CHAPEL (➤ 23, TOP TEN)

ST ABBS ✪✪✪

St Abbs is a working fishing village. You can take a boat trip to get a closer look at the guillemots, kittiwakes, fulmars and razorbills which sweep and squeal and nest around the surrounding rocks and cliffs. Diving, to view the spectacular underwater scenery and sea life in these clear waters, is also possible. The nature reserve, close to the village, offers rock-pool rambles and armchair dives, or you can follow the footpath to the lighthouse to appreciate the wonderful coastline and bird life.

TRAQUAIR HOUSE (➤ 26, TOP TEN)

Edinburgh & Borders Drive

From Princes Street head east along Waterloo Place and Regent Road, then turn right into London Road (A1). Follow it until you see signs for Haddington (► 40). Turn right and when your visit is completed, return to the A1 and follow the signs for Berwick-upon-Tweed. After 32km (20 miles), turn left on to the A1107 for Eyemouth, then at Coldingham take a left on to the B6438 to St Abbs (► 42). Return via the B6438 to the A1, then turn left and continue until the turn-off for Duns on the A6105.

Distance
265km (165 miles)

Time
6–8 hours, depending on stops

Start/end point
Edinburgh
✚ 55D4

Lunch
Tontine Hotel, High Street, Peebles (after Innerleithen)

Chirnside, which you will pass, was the home of local farmer Jim Clark (1936–68) who was the world motor racing champion twice in the 1960s. Duns, the next town, has a museum dedicated to his life (44 Newtown Street).

From Duns follow the A6105 to its junction with the A68, turn left and then in a short distance right on to the A6091 until Galashiels, where you turn left on to the A72.

At Innerleithen you will find Robert Smails Printing Works (► 42), and near by is Traquair House (► 26).

Continue on the A72 until it joins the A702 just beyond Skirling. Turn left for Biggar.

In Biggar is the last gas works in Scotland, preserved as a museum; Gladstone Court, an indoor museum of old shops; and the Biggar Puppet Theatre (► 111).

Leave Biggar (A702) heading back the way you came, signed Edinburgh. After 29km (18 miles), turn right on to the A766 for Penicuik.

Here you will find the Edinburgh Crystal Visitors' Centre.

Take the A701 from Penicuik, follow the signs for Roslin village and Rosslyn Chapel (► 23), then return to the A701 and follow the signs back to Edinburgh.

St Abbs Head is a paradise for bird-watchers and naturalists

Glasgow & the Southwest

Glasgow is a fine Victorian city, built on the fortunes of the British Empire. Edinburgh may be the capital of Scotland but Glasgow is its soul. The inhabitants are compulsively outgoing and gregarious so this is not a city to visit if you want to be alone. Sit on a park bench in George Square and within minutes someone will engage you in conversation.

In this area you will find the industrial heart of Scotland, the shipyards of the Clyde, fast-moving computer production, sleepy rural backwaters, the wildernesses of Galloway and miles of coastline. It is a microcosm of Scottish industry, history and literature. Two popular poets, penicillin, tarmacadam, the mackintosh, the bicycle and the pneumatic tyre, not to mention Robert the Bruce and William Wallace, all emerged from the southwest of Scotland.

> *'O beautiful city of Glasgow I must conclude my lay, by calling thee the greatest city of the present day; For your treatment of me was by no means churlish, Therefore I say, 'let Glasgow flourish.'*

WILLIAM TOPAZ MCGONAGAL

The glass-roofed interior of Glasgow's Argyll Arcade built in 1827

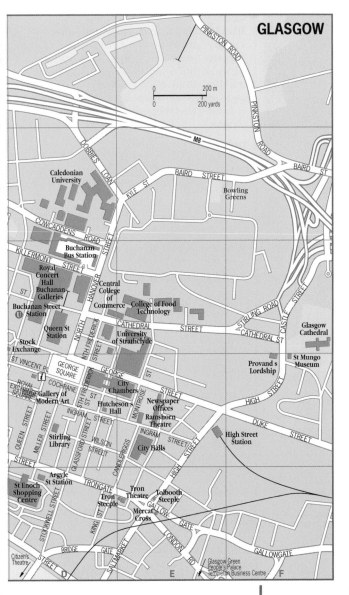

GLASGOW

200 m
200 yards

PINKSTON ROAD
PINKSTON ROAD
M8
BAIRD STREET
BAIRD ST
DOBBIES LOAN
KYLE ST
Caledonian University
Bowling Greens
COWCADDENS ROAD
KILLERMONT STREET
Buchanan Bus Station
Royal Concert Hall
Buchanan Galleries
Buchanan Street Station
HANOVER STREET
Central College of Commerce
College of Food Technology
STIRLING ROAD
Queen St Station
NORTH FREDERICK STREET
CATHEDRAL STREET
CASTLE STREET
Glasgow Cathedral
Stock Exchange
University of Strathclyde
CATHEDRAL ST
St Mungo Museum
ST VINCENT PL
NTH FREDERICK STREET
GEORGE SQUARE
GEORGE STREET
Provand's Lordship
HIGH STREET
ROYAL EXCHANGE SQUARE
COCHRANE ST
City Chambers
MONTROSE ST
Newspaper Offices
DUKE STREET
Gallery of Modern Art
5TH FREDERICK ST
INGRAM STREET
Hutcheson's Hall
Ramshorn Theatre
High Street Station
QUEEN STREET
MILLER STREET
Stirling Library
GLASSFORD STREET
WILSON STREET
INGRAM STREET
City Halls
CANDLERIGGS
HIGH STREET
STREET
Argyle St Station
TRONGATE
Tron Theatre
St Enoch Shopping Centre
STOCKWELL STREET
KING ST
Tron Steeple
Tolbooth Steeple
GALLOWGATE
Mercat Cross
SALTMARKET
LONDON RD
GALLOWGATE
Citizen's Theatre
BRIDGE GATE
Glasgow Green
People's Palace
Templeton Business Centre

D E F

Above: *students at Glasgow School of Art*
Right: *Kelvingrove Art Gallery and Museum is closed for refurbishment until 2006*

47D2
Queen Street
0141 229 1996
Mon–Thu and Sat 10–5, Fri and Sun from 11
Excellent café (£) on premises
Free

46B4
167 Renfrew Street
0141 353 4526
Guided tours Mon–Fri 11, 2, Sat 10:30, 11:30; additional tours Jul, Aug Sat 1, Sun 10:30, 11:30, 1
Mackintosh's Willow Tea Room (£) is near by at 217 Sauchiehall Street
Moderate

Glasgow

Since its portrayal in Alexander MacArthur and Kingsley Long's novel *No Mean City* as a wild, gangster-dominated place, Glasgow has reinvented itself several times. The Garden Festival transformed the derelict dock areas along the Clyde, while The European City of Culture and City of Architecture 1999 proclaimed the stylishness of Glasgow.

World renowned architects such as Charles Rennie Mackintosh and Alexander 'Greek' Thomson produced what has become one of Europe's best preserved Victorian cities. Imaginative modern designs, including the Burrell Collection and the Armadillo, maintain the standard while 1960s and 1970s architectural blight gradually disappears.

What to See in Glasgow

BURRELL COLLECTION (► 17, TOP TEN)

GALLERY OF MODERN ART ⭐⭐

This popular and witty gallery has undermined even the worthy statue of Wellington which fronts it. The great man and his horse are constantly adorned with traffic cones for headgear. In the entrance, the irreverent tone is set by the brilliant, papier mâché caricature of the Queen as a Glasgow housewife, in dressing gown and slippers, with dangling cigarette and copy of *Sporting Life*. The city's collection of art by living artists is housed on four floors.

GLASGOW SCHOOL OF ART ⭐⭐⭐

Charles Rennie Mackintosh won the competition to design the new school in 1896. It is the earliest example in the UK of a complete art nouveau building, including all the interior furnishings and fittings. Students today still remove books from Mackintosh bookcases and sit on priceless Mackintosh chairs to study them.

> ### DID YOU KNOW?
>
> The Glasgow Underground, dubbed the Clockwork Orange because of the colour of the trains, is still the best way to get around the city.

HOLMWOOD HOUSE

Recently restored by the National Trust for Scotland, Holmwood House, designed by Alexander 'Greek' Thomson, is one of Scotland's finest private villas. The paper magnate James Couper gave Thomson a free hand and he devised an astonishing asymmetrical design. One side has a flat classical frontage with pillars framing the dining-room windows while the bay window on the other side is essentially a circular Greek temple, complete with free-standing pillars, fronting a timber and glass wall. None of the furniture remains but underneath the layers of paper, a remarkable amount of the original paint scheme has survived, including painted scenes of the Trojan Wars.

✚ 46C1
✉ 61 Netherlee Road, Cathcart
☎ 0141 637 2129
🕐 Apr–Oct daily 12–5
🍴 Refreshments in Kitchen Court (£)
✋ Cheap
🚌 44, 66
🚉 Glasgow Central (Neilston train to Cathcart station)

KELVINGROVE ART GALLERY AND MUSEUM

This elaborately turreted mansion, built of red Dumfriesshire sandstone on the banks of the River Kelvin, is currently closed for refurbishment (► panel). Its art collection includes works by Botticelli, the Pre-Raphaelites, the Impressionists and David Hockney, as well as many great Scottish artists, such as the Glasgow Boys (► 57). The museum has collections ranging from Egyptology and prehistory to ship-building and natural history.

✚ 46A4
✉ Argyll Street
☎ 0141 287 2699
🕐 Closed for major refurbishment until 2006. During this time the core of the art collection will be on display in the McLellan Galleries in Sauchiehall Street

MUSEUM OF TRANSPORT

Glasgow's transport museum displays the entire history of Scottish transport, including the pioneer days of the Scottish motor industry. Cars include early Arrol Johnstones produced in Dumfries and the Hillman Imp, built at the long-closed Chrysler plant at Linwood. There is also a whole series of trams, the famous 'Shooglies', the earlier ones resplendent in gleaming brass and polished wood, as well as an entire 1938 street scene with a working cinema and a Victorian underground station.

✚ 46A4
✉ Argyll Street
☎ 0141 287 2720
🕐 Mon–Sat 10–5, Sun 11–5
✋ Free

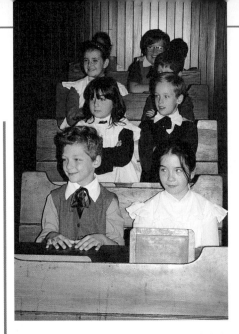

Modern-day students get a taste of Victorian education at Scotland Street School Museum

46A1
225 Scotland Street
0141 287 0500
Mon–Thu and Sat 10–5, Fri and Sun 11–5
Good café on premises (£)
Free

SCOTLAND STREET SCHOOL MUSEUM ✪✪✪

Designed by Charles Rennie Mackintosh, this is an architectural gem, featuring two massive glass-fronted towers. Inside it re-creates the school experience of Scots children from Victorian times through to the 1950s. Classrooms have been reconstructed for several of the periods and in term time visitors in the viewing galleries can watch local children and their teachers dress up in period costume and experience first-hand what it was like. Modern-day kids sometimes feel a little strange as their familiar, friendly teacher is transformed into the fire-breathing dragon of the Victorian classroom. At play time the youngsters take part in games from yesteryear. There are wooden spinning tops, jauries (an old type of marble) and girds and cleeks (hoops and sticks). The only problem for the children is capturing the toys from the grown-ups.

46A3
Yorkhill Quay, 100 Stobcross Road
0141 339 0631
Daily 10–dusk
Café (£)
Moderate

THE TALL SHIP AT GLASGOW HARBOUR ✪✪✪

The River Clyde dominated world ship-building well into the 20th century. Many of the legendary liners, the *Queen Mary*, *Queen Elizabeth* and the *QE2*, were built here as well as other less famous ships. The *Glenlee* (1896) is one of the last of the Clyde-built sailing ships and one of only six still afloat. It was in the service of the Spanish navy until the 1970s. Acquired by the Clyde Maritime Trust, who have spent years restoring it, this steel-hulled cargo ship is one of Glasgow's newest attractions.

THE TENEMENT HOUSE, GLASGOW (► 25, TOP TEN)

Glasgow Walk

This walk around the centre of the city takes in some interesting buildings and architecture.

From the tourist office in George Square turn right then right into Miller Street, left along Ingram Street and right into Glassford Street.

The Tobacco Lairds House is in Miller Street. Glasgow's oldest secular building is the Trades Hall in Glassford Street, designed by Robert Adam in 1794.

Turn left into Wilson Street, right at Candleriggs and left along the Trongate. Turn right on to Saltmarket and left into Glasgow Green. Follow the paths to the People's Palace and beyond that to Templeton Business Centre.

Modelled on the Palazzo Ducale in Venice, the multi-coloured, richly patterned Templeton Business Centre was originally a Victorian carpet factory.

Return to the gates of Glasgow Green and go along Clyde Street. Turn right into Jamaica Street, right into Howard Street and left into St Enoch Square. Across Argyle Street head along Buchanan Street. Walk around Royal Exchange Square on the right. Continue on Buchanan Street then left along St Vincent Street.

In St Enoch Square the former underground station resembles a miniature château. St Vincent Street Church is the only surviving church of the Victorian architect Alexander 'Greek' Thomson.

Turn right up Pitt Street and right into Renfrew Street, right at Dalhousie Street and left along Sauchiehall Street.

In Sauchiehall Street is another Thomson design, the former Grecian Chambers, and the Willow Tea Rooms, owned by Kate Cranston.

At Buchanan Street turn right, then left along West George Street to return to George Square.

Distance
5–6km (3–4 miles)

Time
4 hours

Start/end point
George Square
✠ 47D2

Lunch
78 St Vincent Street
☎ 0141 248 7878

The Willow, Glasgow, last remnant of Kate Cranston's famous tea-room, designed by Mackintosh at the end of the 19th century

What to See in the Southwest

🔲 54A4

🍴 Excellent cafés in Brodick (£)

🚢 Caledonian MacBrayne Ferry from Gourock

The triangular design of 13th-century Caerlaverock Castle is unique

ARRAN ⭐

Reached by Calmac Ferry from Gourock, the island of Arran is a delight. The main town of Brodick with its castle and gardens can be explored in a day-trip. But a few days are necessary to visit the standing stones on Machrie Moor, climb Goatfell or watch the sunset over Ailsa Craig from the south coast. Pottery, paintings, textiles, basketwork and glass, as well as cheese and whisky, are produced locally.

BURNS NATIONAL HERITAGE PARK (► 16, TOP TEN)

🔲 55D2

✉ Near Bankend on B725 19km (12 miles) south of Dumfries

☎ 01387 770200

🕐 Daily 10–5

🚌 371 from Dumfries

💷 Cheap

CAERLAVEROCK CASTLE AND WILDFOWL AND ⭐ WETLANDS TRUST RESERVE

Thirteenth-century Caerlaverock Castle, dramatically sited on the estuary of the River Nith, is the only triangular castle in Scotland. Built of red sandstone, with an imposing double towered gatehouse, it was protected by a moat and huge ramparts. The castle was besieged, damaged and rebuilt by Scottish and English alike, and changed hands many times over the centuries, particularly during the Wars of Independence (1296–1328). Inside there are the remains of a fine Renaissance mansion house built around 1620. It was finally left a ruin by the depredations of the Covenanters (Scots Protestants) a few years later. Further along the Solway is the Wildfowl and Wetlands Trust Reserve where acres of Merseland (mud flats and salt marshes) are conserved to protect the wildlife and to allow visitors to observe from hides without disturbing the environment. Caerlaverock is home to the most northerly

> ### DID YOU KNOW?
> The Paddle Steamer *Waverley* which used to take thousands of Glaswegians to Clyde resorts such as Rothesay and Dunoon still makes the nostalgic trip 'doon the watter'. You can wine, dine and dance as the steamer sails into a summer sunset over the islands of the Firth of Clyde.

colony of natterjack toads, and every summer the entire Spitsbergen colony of barnacle geese arrives. There are plenty of activities for people of all ages, from bat-watching evenings to pond dipping.

CULZEAN CASTLE AND COUNTRY PARK ✪✪✪

Perched on a cliff top over the Firth of Clyde, Culzean was constructed for the 10th Earl of Cassillis by the architect Robert Adam. It took 20 years to complete and was finally finished in 1792. Built in neo-Gothic style, with towers and turrets on the outside, the classical design of the inside is dominated by the majestic oval staircase. During his lifetime, the former US President Dwight D Eisenhower had the use of the top floor, and his life and work are commemorated in a permanent display. The castle is set in an extensive country park with gardens, sea-shore, wooded walks and a pond where elegant swans are reflected in its glassy green.

🔲 54B3
✉ 19km (12 miles) southwest of Ayr on A719
☎ 01655 884400
🕐 Apr–Oct 10:30–5. Park: daily 9–sunset
🍴 Tea room in park (££)
♿ Moderate

Culzean Castle gardens, part of Scotland's first country park

SOUTHERN SCOTLAND

Dunfermline
Kirkcaldy
FIFE
M90
Burntisland
Bo'ness
Inverkeithing
South Queensferry
Linlithgow
Firth of Forth
North Berwick
Bass Rock
Tantallon Castle
Gullane
Dunbar
EDINBURGH
Musselburgh
Haddington
East Linton
Cockburnspath
St Abb's Head
M8
Livingston
C EDIN
EAST LOTHIAN
Coldingham
St Abbs
Eyemouth
WEST LOTHIAN
Rosslyn Chapel
Dalkeith
Bonnyrigg
Grantshouse
MID-LOTHIAN
533m
Penicuik
Chirnside
Berwick-upon-Tweed
Pentland Hills
West Linton
Moorfoot Hills
Uplands
Lammermuir Hills
Duns
Swinton
Peebles
Lauder
Stow
Coldstream
659m
Innerleithen
Galashiels
Kelso
Tweed
Biggar
Robert Smail's Printing Works
Traquair House
Melrose
Wooler
Upper Tweeddale
Abbotsford House
St Boswells
Tweed
Selkirk
Ancrum
Town Yetholm
SCOTTISH BORDERS
Jedburgh
Denholm
822m
Ettrick
Teviotdale
Hawick
The Cheviot Hills
White Coomb
Carter Bar
Moffat
Samye Ling Tibetan Centre
Teviothead
Otterburn
Eskdalemuir
Esk
Boreland
Liddel
A74M
Newcastleton
Annan
Lochmaben
Lockerbie
Langholm
Ecclefechan
Corbridge
Glencaple
Gretna Green
Caerlaverock Castle
Annan
Brampton
Hexham
Nith Estuary
Carlisle
Consett
ENGLAND
M6
Cockermouth
Penrith
Workington
D
E
F

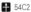 54C2

Burns House Museum
- ✉ Burns Street
- ☎ 01387 255297
- 🕐 Apr–Sep, Mon–Sat 10–5, Sun 2–5; Oct–Mar, Tue–Sat 10–1, 2–5
- 🍴 Several excellent cafés and eateries (£) in town
- ♿ Free

Above: *Devorgilla's Bridge over the River Nith at Dumfries*

 54B3
- ✉ Dalmellington Road Waterside Patna
- ☎ 01292 531144
- 🕐 Daily Apr–Oct 10–5 and by request in winter
- 🍴 Restaurant and coffee shop on premises (£)
- ♿ Moderate
- 🚌 51 from Ayr

54B2
- 🍴 Cafés and tea rooms (£) at various villages and towns throughout the park

DUMFRIES ✪✪

This quiet county town was home to two of Scotland's literary greats, Robert Burns and J M Barrie. Robert Burns, after an unsuccessful farming venture at nearby Ellisland, moved to Dumfries and worked as an Excise man until his untimely death. His house is now a **museum** and on display are the bed he died in and the desk where he copied the words of *Auld Lang Syne*. In the Globe Inn, visitors can sit in the poet's chair but must recite a verse of his poetry or buy the assembled company a drink.

J M Barrie finished his schooling at Dumfries Academy, and it was while playing pirates with his friends in a garden next to the school that Peter Pan was born. The garden was the inspiration for Never Never Land and Captain Hook was his maths master. In Dumfries Museum the earliest example of Barrie's writing can be seen.

DUNASKIN OPEN AIR MUSEUM ✪✪✪

This is the best preserved Victorian ironworks in Europe. Sited in the countryside, close to the Ayrshire coal fields, it survived because there was no need to demolish it for the space. There are delightful walks through Dunaskin Glen, a period cottage and an opportunity to experience working in a coal mine. An audio-visual re-creates Ayrshire life in the 19th and early 20th centuries and there are lots of hands-on activities for children.

GALLOWAY FOREST PARK AND ✪✪✪
GLENTROOL

The Galloway Forest Park centred around lovely Loch Trool and the Galloway Hills is an area of outstanding natural beauty. Hill-walking in this empty wilderness is rewarded by splendid views over lochs, hills and coast. Less strenuous is a stroll or cycle through the myriad forest paths or a drive along the Queen's Way to the pretty village of New Galloway.

KIRKCUDBRIGHT ⊕⊕

There is a magic quality to the light in this part of the world that draws artists to set up home. The illustrator Jessie M King and her husband, E A Taylor, lived at Green Gate Close in High Street, while Edward Hornel, one of the Glasgow Boys, a group of Scottish painters inspired by the Impressionists, lived near by at **Broughton House** (house closed for renovation 2003). Hornel's Georgian mansion, with its Japanese garden, is now a museum to his life and work. In the Old Tolbooth is an art centre featuring the work of local artists. Also worth a visit is the Stewartry Museum and MacLellan's Castle, which dominates the square beside the picturesque working harbour.

⊞ 54C1

Broughton House
⊠ High Street
☎ 01557 330437
🕐 House closed for
   renovation 2003. Garden:
   Feb–Mar and 1–20 Oct
   Mon–Fri 11–4; Apr–Sep
   Mon–Sat 11–5, Sun 1–5

St Ninian's Priory Church, Whithorn

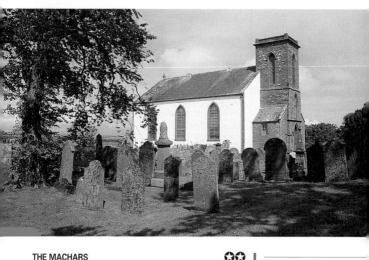

THE MACHARS ⊕⊕

This peninsula south of Newton Stewart is a time warp, reminiscent of the Sunday afternoons of yesteryears. Wigtown, once a prosperous and bustling county town, used to look and feel like a ghost town. Now, as Scotland's official book town, it has been given a new lease of life and is gradually regaining something of its former glory.

Further south is the sleepy town of Whithorn, where Chrisitianity first came to Scotland with St Ninian in AD 397. Pilgrims flocked here from all over the Christian world until pilgrimage was banned during the Reformation. Much of medieval Whithorn remains, and at the **Whithorn Dig** the earlier settlements are being excavated.

⊞ 54B1

Whithorn Dig
⊠ George Street
☎ 01988 500508
🕐 Apr–Oct, daily 10:30–5
🍴 Tea room near by (£)
👢 Cheap

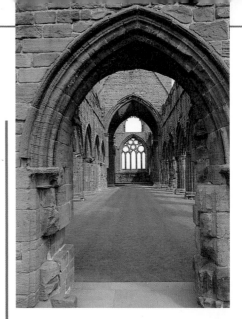

Sweetheart Abbey, last resting place of the hearts of Devorgilla de Balliol and her husband

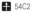 54C2

Sweetheart Abbey
- New Abbey
- 01387 850397
- Apr–Sep, daily 9:30–6:30; Oct–Mar, Mon–Wed and Sat 9:30–4.30, Thu 9:30–12:30, Sun 2–4:30
- The excellent New Abbey Tea Room is adjacent (£)
- Cheap
- 372 from Dumfries

NEW ABBEY ✪✪

Nestling under the shadow of Criffel, the village of New Abbey is dominated by the ruins of a Cistercian abbey. It was founded in 1273 by Devorgilla de Balliol, wife of the Scottish king John Balliol, founder of Balliol College, Oxford and became known as **Sweetheart Abbey** because the hearts of Devorgilla and her husband are interred together here.

New Abbey Cornmill is a water-driven mill in the care of the National Trust for Scotland, with working machinery. Close to New Abbey is the museum of costume and dress at Shambellie House, and at Arbigland, near the village of Kirkbean, is the cottage birthplace of John Paul Jones (1747–92), founder of the United States Navy.

If the sky is clear a climb to Criffel's peak, 570m, will provide a view into four kingdoms – Scotland, Ireland, England and the Isle of Man.

NEW LANARK (▶ 22, TOP TEN)

 55D3
- Eskdalemuir
- 01387 373232
- Daily
- Café on site (£)
- Free
- 112 from Langholm

SAMYE LING TIBETAN CENTRE ✪✪

Probably the last thing you would expect to find in this remote and lonely corner of Dumfries and Galloway is a Buddhist monastery. Yet here it is in all its splendour. Elaborate oriental buildings in bright red and gold sit high up in the Southern Uplands of Scotland with the tranquil sounds of wind chimes filling the air. Tibetan monks built Samye Ling, but it is home to a community of Buddhists. There are various courses in meditation on offer, including weekend workshops and retreats, and visitors are very welcome.

The Southwest Drive

This drive will take you through some of the finest scenery in Scotland – rugged mountains, rocky coastline, low-lying pastures and picturesque towns and villages.

From Dumfries follow the A710 via New Abbey, Kirkbean and Colvend to Dalbeattie.

The John Paul Jones birthplace museum near Kirkbean (➤ 58) is a tribute to the Scot who founded the American Navy. New Abbey is the site of Sweetheart Abbey (➤ 58).

From Dalbeattie take the A711 to Kirkcudbright, then the A762 to New Galloway.

Tiny Palnackie is the venue for the annual World Flounder Tramping Championships. Here competitors stand in the water, waiting until they feel a flounder moving under their feet, then reach down and scoop the fish up. At Dundrennan is another ruined abbey.

From New Galloway turn right on to the A712 to Balmaclellan, then the B7075 and right on to the A702 to Moniaive.

The clogmaker at Balmaclellan welcomes visitors to his workshop, while the picturesque village of Moniaive has a series of leafleted walks and the Green Tea House, an organic café.

Take the B729 just beyond Kirkland to Dunscore, then turn right on to a local road heading towards Newtonairds and follow the signs for Shawhead.

At Glenkiln Reservoir, a collection of sculptures by Henry Moore, Jacob Epstein and Auguste Rodin is displayed in the sweeping pastoral landscape. Moore's King and Queen sculpture on the hillside overlooking the reservoir has become the symbol of Glenkiln.

From Glenkiln continue along the side of the reservoir to Shawhead; follow the local road to the A75, turn left and return to Dumfries.

Distance
153km (95 miles)

Time
6–8 hours depending on stops

Start/end point
Dumfries
✛ 54C2

Lunch
Craigdarroch Arms,
Moniaive (£)

Ancient carvings in the ruins of Dundrennan Abbey

Food & Drink

Traditional Scottish cooking can be a culinary delight, but perseverance is required to find good examples. The poor diet of many Scots has dubbed Scotland the heart attack capital of Europe. Avoid the deep-fried Mars bar, but a fish supper (fish in batter with chips) can be good, especially in fishing areas.

Smoked Scottish salmon – just add lemon juice

Food for a Parliament
Kinfauns Castle (➤ 97) in Perthshire, the magnificent setting of regular Gourmet Evenings, is one of the best places in Scotland to enjoy fresh Scottish produce, cooked with traditional skills and continental flare. Its head chef, Jeremy Wares, Restaurant Chef of the Year 1999, was one of the top chefs chosen to cook a gourmet Scottish dinner for the opening of the Scottish Parliament in 1999.

Fish

As a fishing nation, the traditional food of the poor was tatties and herring (boiled potatoes with herring in oatmeal). The Arbroath smokie, whole haddock smoked in the traditional way, is the gourmet smoked fish, delicious cooked with milk and butter. Avoid the vivid deep-dyed yellow of the chemically processed smoked haddock. Cullen skink, a soup made from smoked haddock, potatoes, onions and cream, is practically a meal in itself. Salmon is readily available since the increase in fish farming, but wild salmon can be found at good fishmongers. It may cost more but the taste is superb.

Meat

Haggis is the best-known Scottish meat dish, made from sheep offal, blood, spices and oatmeal and boiled in a sheep's stomach. If that makes you squeamish you can get a vegetarian version, made from nuts and pulses.

Traditionally it is eaten with mashed tatties (potatoes) and neeps (turnips) but Stac Polly restaurants in Edinburgh serve haggis in filo pastry with plum sauce. The traditional dish to serve at New Year is steak pie. Good butchers make their own steak pies, which have flaky pastry and a rich gravy, and mutton pies with thin, dry pastry filled with minced meat.

Oat Cuisine and Dining Out

A traditional Scottish breakfast starts with porridge, (► panel) followed by eggs, bacon, square slice (a kind of beef sausage), black pudding (a spicy blood pudding), potato scones and tomatoes. This comes with copious quantities of tea, buttered rolls and marmalade. If you need lunch after this, pick up a midday snack of Scotch Broth or pie and beans in a pub or café.

For eating out in the evening, there are many excellent restaurants specialising in traditional and imaginative Scottish menus. A typical menu might start with smoked salmon or partan bree (crab soup), serve high-quality Aberdeen Angus or game as a main course and finish off with the luxurious cranachan, a dish which combines toasted oatmeal with raspberries, cream, honey and whisky. Before or after the pudding, local cheeses such as Dunsyre Blue or Dunlop might be served with oatcakes. Traditionally, fine food is accompanied by French wine but to round off the evening try Drambuie, a whisky-based liqueur made from a secret recipe originating with Bonnie Prince Charlie.

The National Drink

Whisky, Scotland's national drink is distilled from barley. There are hundreds of malt whiskies, aged for 10 or 12 years, sometimes more in wooden casks. The flavour of each malt reflects the spring water, the peat, the type of cask and the years of maturation. Most pubs have a selection of the better-known malts.

Advertised as 'Scotland's other national drink', Irn-Bru is a sickly orange-coloured fizzy drink, reputed to cure hangovers. There could be no other reason for drinking it.

Oats

Oatmeal is a staple Scottish ingredient. Porridge, made by cooking oatmeal in water or milk, is eaten salted, sometimes with cream, never with sugar. In times past, cooked porridge would be poured into the bottom drawer of a dresser, then cut into slices and eaten cold. Oatcakes are made from oatmeal flour and butter. The mass-produced version tastes like cardboard, but there are dozens of small local producers making delicious variations.

Haggis, 'Great chieftain o' the Puddin' race!'

Central Scotland

This disparate cross-section of Scotland stretches from the lonely island-scattered western coastline of Argyll and the Hebrides to the fishing villages of the East Neuk of Fife on the Firth of Forth, all the way to the silvery Tay, Angus and the featureless expanse of the North Sea beyond. It includes wild hills, moorlands and waterways, the bustling small towns of Scotland's central belt and lush agricultural land.

Rising in the great central plain is the rocky prominence of Stirling Castle, which saw some of the fiercest fighting in the Scottish Wars of Independence (1296–1328), while further north lie the refined country town of Perth, down-to-earth Dundee and the heather-covered splendour of the Angus Glens.

> *'And far abin the Angus straths I*
> *saw the wild geese flee,*
> *A lang, lang skein o beatin wings*
> *wi their heids toward the sea,*
> *And aye their cryin voices trailed*
> *ahint them on the air.'*
> *'Oh wind, hae mercy, haud your*
> *wheesht for I daurna listen mair.'*

VIOLET JACOB
1915

Dundee

Dundee straggles untidily along the River Tay, its two distinctive bridges reaching out long thin highways of road and rail over the broad stretch of water to Fife. Of the three Js – jute, jam and journalism – which were the lifeblood of the town, only journalism remains, in the shape of D C Thomson, who publish the *Dandy* and the *Beano* comics and the *Sunday Post*. In the surrounding countryside, the many berry fields which used to supply the jam factories now allow you to pick your own fruit. The town has reinvented itself as a popular conference centre, assisted by the unassuming friendliness of the people. This, together with the unpretentious cultural life, excellent museums and small theatres, make it an agreeable base for touring the area.

Captain Scott's ship Discovery, Dundee's premier tourist attraction

What to See in Dundee

BROUGHTY FERRY AND CASTLE ✪

Broughty Ferry, once a separate village, is now a suburb of Dundee. It is popular with Dundonians and visitors alike, with its eclectic mix of restaurants, pubs and shops and sandy beach along the banks of the silvery Tay. Fifteenth-century **Broughty Castle**, now a museum, tells the story of Broughty Ferry and the whaling industry.

RRS *DISCOVERY* AND ✪✪✪
HM FRIGATE *UNICORN*

Once the pride of the Panmuir yard, where she was built in 1901 for the polar expeditions of Captain Robert Falcon Scott, the **Royal Research Ship** *Discovery* lay rotting for years on the Thames Embankment in London. Finally returned to her birthplace, restored, and housed at the purpose-built Discovery Point, she is now a major tourist attraction.

The Frigate *Unicorn*, further along the Tay at Victoria Dock, is the oldest British warship still afloat. Built in 1824, she was, incredibly, still in service until 1968.

✚ 79E2

Broughty Castle
☎ 01382 436916
🕐 Tue–Sat 11–5, Sun 12:30–4; closed Mon Oct–Mar 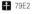 Free

---

✚ 79E2

RRS *Discovery*
✉ Victoria Quay, near the Tay Bridge
☎ 01382 201245
🕐 Apr–Oct, Mon–Sat 10–5, Sun 11–5; Nov–Mar, Mon–Sat 10–4, Sun 11–4
🍴 Café (£)
♿ Very good
🎫 Moderate

79E2

⊠ Albert Square, city centre

☎ 01382 432084

◷ Mon–Sat 10–5, (until 7 Thu), Sun 12:30–4

🍴 Café (£)

♿ Very good

🆓 Free

MCMANUS ART GALLERY AND MUSEUM ✪

This is an absolute gem of a place, one of the finest Victorian buildings in Dundee, and that's just the outside. Indoors, the museum covers Dundee's history from the ancient Picts to modern times. There's also a great display on the Tay Bridge disaster. On 28 December, 1879, the bridge collapsed in a storm after only 18 months, and 75 people died. Upstairs in the Albert Hall, with its pitch pine-panelled roof, are collections of glass, gold, silver, musical instruments and furniture, including the table where the death warrants for captured Jacobites were signed by the Duke of Cumberland after the Battle of Culloden in 1746. The art collection in the Victoria Gallery includes several Scottish collections and some superb Pre-Raphaelites.

 79E2

⊠ Balgay Park. Approach via Perth Road, Blackness Avenue, Balgay Road

☎ 01382 435846

◷ Apr–Sep, Tue–Fri 11–5, Sat, Sun 12:30–4; Oct–Mar, Mon–Fri 4–10, Sat, Sun 12:30–4

♿ Few

🆓 Free

❓ Booking essential for large groups and for Planetarium

MILLS OBSERVATORY ✪✪

This is the only public observatory in Britain, and the enthusiastic and knowledgeable resident astronomer is a delight to talk to. There are special openings for eclipses and the odd visiting comet. Winter evenings are obviously the best time to go, but in the summer months, when it's light, there are exhibits and displays well worth seeing.

McManus Art Gallery, Victorian splendour in Dundee

VERDANT WORKS ✪✪

Verdant Works was one of Dundee's many jute mills which produced hessian and sacking, and once employed 50,000 people locally; it has been restored and reconstructed as a museum. Volunteers operate textile machines, while 'Juteopolis', a 15-minute film, explains the dramatic impact of the industry on the city and its people. Every day at 1PM the works' 'bummer' (factory whistle) is blown, a sound that marked the livelihood of many families in Dundee and recalls its history in an evocative way.

 79E2

⊠ 27 West Henderson's Wynd

☎ 01382 225282

🚶 Apr–Oct 10–5; Nov–Mar 10:30–4

🍴 Refreshments (£)

♿ Very good

🆓 Expensive

Central Scotland Drive

Start from Perth. Take the A85, then turn right on to the A93 and right again on to the A94. (Scone Palace is 2.5km/1½ miles further along the A93.) At Balbeggie, take the B953 to Inchture, then turn left on to the A90. Take the A85 left through Dundee, past Discovery Point and follow the signs for the Tay Bridge and the A92. Pass through Newport-on-Tay and Leuchars to St Andrews, then follow the A917. Follow the coastline of the East Neuk, diverting through the picturesque villages of Crail, Anstruther, Pittenweem, St Monance and Elie.

From Crail take the B940 to Scotland's Secret Bunker. This underground relic of the Cold War would have become the administrative centre of Scotland in the event of a nuclear attack. It was an official secret until 1994 when it opened to the public. Part of it is still operational.

Turn left on to the A915.

Have a look at Lower Largo, with its statue of Alexander Selkirk, the prototype of Robinson Crusoe. A native of Largo, Selkirk ran away to sea and was marooned on Juan Fernand Island from 1705 to 1709.

Continue on the A91, then turn right on to the A911 and in Glenrothes turn right on to the A92, then left on to the A912. At Falkland follow the B936 to Auchtermuchty and turn left on to the A91. From the A91 turn left on to the B919, left on to the A911, then after Kinnesswood, right on to the B920. At the junction turn right on to the B9097, right again on to the B996 and continue to Kinross.

This route circles Loch Leven with the 14th-century ruins of Loch Leven Castle on an island. Mary, Queen of Scots, was imprisoned here in 1567.

Take the A922 to Milnathort and the B996 via Glenfarg to the A912. Turn left and follow the road through Bridge of Earn back to Perth.

Distance
190km (118 miles)

Time
6–8 hours including stops

Start/end point
Perth
🚑 79D1

Lunch
The Naafi at the Secret Bunker (£)
☎ 0133 310301

Maintaining the fishing fleet in Pittenweem

What to See in Central Scotland

THE ANGUS GLENS ✪✪✪

✚ 79E2

The Glens of Angus are a series of five glorious glens to the north of Dundee. Rich in wildlife and a botanist's paradise, look out particularly for red deer and arctic plants. Glen Clova is probably the most picturesque, and there are several lovely walks to choose from. Jock's Road, which leads through the mountains to Braemar, some 22.5km (14 miles) away, is spectacular. The path clings, precariously at times, to the edge of the hill, the water runs far below and, as you climb, the view of the glen behind falls away in a changing and winding perspective, misty in the distance. Passable only in summer, don't even think about it between October and March.

Below: *Crarae, one of the finest gardens in Scotland*

BO'NESS AND KINNIEL RAILWAY ✪✪

✚ 79D1
✉ Off Union Street, Bo'ness
☎ 01506 822298
🖐 Apr–Oct, every weekend (Jul–Aug Tue–Sun); Santa Specials Dec weekends
🖐 Moderate

This is one of the best of the small independent railway lines, situated in the town of Bo'ness, the largest centre for vintage trains in Scotland. Five kilometres (3 miles) of track leads to Birkhill, where you can visit the Birkhill Clay Mine or stroll in the Avon Gorge before the old steam train departs for the return journey.

CRARAE GARDEN ✪

✚ 78C1
✉ A83, 16km (10 miles) southwest of Inveraray
☎ 01546 886614
🖐 Gardens daily dawn–dusk; visitor centre from 10
🍴 Refreshments (£)
🖐 Moderate

Between Inveraray and Lochgilphead, this garden is laid out round the glen of the Crarae Burn which flows into Loch Fyne. Covering over 20ha, there are two walking routes, the inner and outer circles which both start from the car-park. Strategically placed seats allow you to enjoy majestic views over Loch Fyne while admiring the snowdrops, daffodils, bluebells, azaleas, rhododendrons or magnolias according to season.

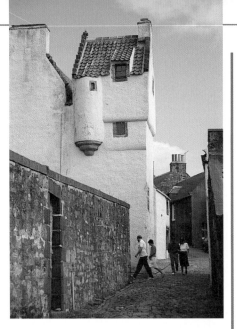

CULROSS AND CULROSS PALACE ✪✪

The National Trust for Scotland tends the red-tiled houses and whitewashed walls of this delightful town. Walk through the cobbled Back Causeway, visit the remains of the Cistercian Culross Abbey, or the Study, a restored 17th-century house. The 16th-century merchant's house known as **Culross Palace** is the main attraction, with little rooms and narrow passages. St Mungo, the founder, and patron saint of Glasgow, was reputedly born here.

EAST NEUK OF FIFE ✪✪✪

The coastline of the East Neuk is dotted with a string of little fishing villages. Quaint cottages with red-tiled roofs and crow-stepped gables perch around secluded harbours. Crail is without a doubt the prettiest, while Anstruther and Pittenweem are still regular working ports. Anstruther is home to the **Scottish Fisheries Museum**, where the entire history of fishing in Scotland unfolds. Kellie Castle, north of Anstruther, is a restored 16th-century building with a garden full of delightful nooks and crannies.

THE FALKIRK WHEEL EXPERIENCE ✪✪✪

Designed to connect the Forth and Clyde and Union canals, this massive rotating boat lift carries eight boats at a time and is fast becoming a top attraction. The state-of-the-art visitor centre tells the story of the Wheel and the history of canals. Boat trips from the visitor centre sail on to the Wheel which ascends to join the Union Canal 35 metres (115ft) above. The journey continues along the canal by the historic Antonine Wall before returning.

✚ 79D1
✉ 12km (7½ miles) west of Dunfermline

Culross Palace
☎ 01383 880359
🕐 Apr–Sep, daily 12–5
🍴 Café (£)
♿ Moderate

✚ 79E1

Scottish Fisheries Museum
✉ Anstruther Harbour
☎ 01333 310628
🕐 Mon–Sat 10–4:30, Sun 11–4
🍴 Tea room (£)
♿ Moderate

✚ 79D1
✉ Lime Road, Tamfourhill, Falkirk
☎ 01324 619888
🕐 Visitor Centre: Apr–Oct 9–6:30 (winter 10–5)
♿ Visitor Centre: free; boat trip: expensive

78C1

Hill House
✉ Upper Colquhoun Street
☎ 01436 673900
⏰ Apr–Oct 1:30–5:30
🍴 Tea room (£)
♿ Moderate

Opposite: *Inveraray
Castle, seat of the
Dukes of Argyll*

78B2

*Tobermory harbour with
its gaily coloured cottages*

HELENSBURGH AND HILL HOUSE ⭐⭐⭐

The main attraction in this attractive Georgian town on the Firth of Clyde is **Hill House**, designed by Charles Rennie Mackintosh in 1902 for the publisher Walter Blackie. Mackintosh was given a completely free hand in the design of the house, its interior and furnishings. The result is one of the finest art nouveau houses in Britain, now painstakingly restored by The National Trust for Scotland. The exterior echoes a traditional tower with its irregular windows, round turret and solid expanses of wall. Inside, it is light and elegant with perfect proportions and delightful glimpses of the adjoining spaces as you move through it.

Henry Bell, the inventor of the *Comet*, an early steam-driven boat, was bathing master in Helensburgh, which was also the birthplace of the inventor of television, John Logie Baird.

THE INNER HEBRIDES ⭐⭐

There's a magical quality about the islands of Islay, Jura, Mull, Iona, Coll and Tiree. Most tourists head for Tobermory on Mull, with its gaily coloured houses fronting the harbour where, tradition has it, the wreck of a Spanish galleon lies laden with gold. Iona, with its mighty cathedral and connections with St Columba, draws pilgrims from all over the world. Jura has wonderful, blindingly white, sandy beaches that are all but deserted – just the spot to get away from it all. But it is to Islay that you must go if you want to experience some of the finest whiskies in Scotland. Islay malts are unique and easily distinguished by their smokey, peaty taste.

INVERARAY ⊕⊕

This small 18th-century town, built by the Duke of Argyll, clan chief of the Campbells, has an enchanting view over Loch Fyne. The old gaol and adjoining court-house are now a museum. Inveraray Castle, home of the Duke of Argyll, would not be out of place on the Loire. In the stable block the Combined Operations Museum is dedicated to the troops that trained on Loch Fyne for the D-Day landings in Normandy. Inside the castle itself is a collection of weapons given to the Campbells by the government to help repress the Jacobites.

Southwest of Inveraray is the restored township of **Auchindrain**, now a folk museum, with around 20 thatched cottages set up to re-create life prior to the Clearances.

KIRRIEMUIR ⊕⊕

Kirriemuir was the birthplace of J M Barrie, novelist, dramatist and creator of *Peter Pan*. The house he was born in is now a **museum**, and outside is the wash-house, the prototype of the house the Lost Boys built for Wendy, which the young Barrie used as a theatre for his first plays. Barrie is buried in the local cemetery.

LINLITHGOW ⊕⊕

Mary, Queen of Scots, was born here at **Linlithgow Palace** in 1542. Although a royal building had existed here since the time of David I (1124–53), it was James I who built the present one. It survived until 1746 when it was destroyed by fire, but it's well worth a visit. Overlooking Linlithgow Loch, the roofless ruin has spiral staircases, stately rooms, a magnificent Great Hall, and a brewery down below.

🞤 78C1

Auchindrain

✉ 8km (5 miles) southwest of Inveraray

☎ 01499 500235

🕐 Apr–Sep, daily 10–5

🖐 Moderate

🞤 79E2

J M Barrie Musuem

✉ 9 Brechin Road

☎ 01575 572646

🕐 Phone for opening times

🖐 Cheap

🞤 79D1

Linlithgow Palace

✉ South shore of loch

☎ 01506 842896

🕐 Apr–Sep, daily 9:30–6:30; Oct–Mar, Mon–Sat 9:30–4:30, Sun 2–4:30

🖐 Cheap

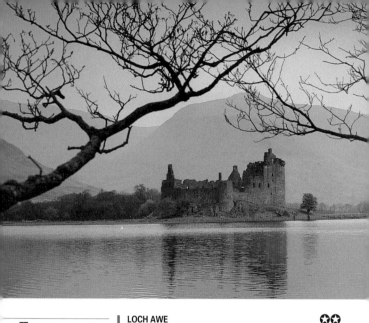

78C1

Bonawe Iron Furnace
- Off the A85 at Bonawe
- 01866 822432
- Mar–Sep, daily 9:30–6:30; Oct–Nov Mon–Sat 9:30–4:30, Sun 2–4
- Cheap

78C1
- Near the marina in Balloch
- Apr–Oct, daily 10–5 (Jul and Aug 9:30–7:30)

Above: *romantic Loch Awe and Kilchurn Castle, a 15th-century Campbell stronghold*

79E2
- 1.5km (1 mile) from Montrose, on the A92
- 01674 676336
- Apr–Oct, daily 10:30–5; Nov–Mar, daily 10:30–4
- Moderate

LOCH AWE ●●
This is the longest freshwater loch in Scotland. There are forest walks at Barnaline, near Dalavich, and near the head of the loch you will find the tiny island of Inishail, with its 13th-century chapel. At Taynuilt, visit the restored industrial heritage centre of **Bonawe Iron Furnace** before heading back towards the loch via the gloomy Pass of Brander for a tour of the Cruachan Power Station. The station is built into Ben Cruachan, where hydroelectricity is generated by water pumped up the mountain from the loch below.

LOCH LOMOND ●●
Loch Lomond is terribly overcrowded during the tourist season but it is one of Scotland's great beauty spots. The pretty village of Luss doubles as the fictional Glendarroch in Scottish Television's soap opera *Take the High Road*. To escape the crowds take one of the many boat trips from Balloch which head round the small islands on the loch, or follow the West Highland Way on the east bank to Balmaha and Rowardennan. This is grand walking country and the starting point to climb Ben Lomond, 972m.

MONTROSE BASIN WILDLIFE CENTRE ●
The Basin is a huge tidal lagoon of mud that is a rich habitat for all manner of wildlife. Humans may hold their noses but to the geese, waders and swans that frequent the basin, grubbing in the smelly mud is a gourmet experience. Telescopes, binoculars and video cameras are strategically placed to enable visitors to watch without disturbing the birds, and there is a regular series of guided walks led by the resident ranger.

OBAN ✪

Oban, the main ferry terminal for Caledonian MacBrayne Ferries, is known as the gateway to the Isles. McCaig's Folly, a granite tower, was built for no real reason on a hill overlooking the town, however, it looks dramatic, particularly when floodlit at night. Outside the town are the ruins of 13th-century **Dunstaffanage Castle**, where Flora MacDonald was imprisoned after assisting in the escape of Bonnie Prince Charlie. The Isle of Kerrera in Oban Bay, with a population of less than 50, is easily reached by passenger ferry. It is a peaceful retreat with great views over to Mull and Jura.

✚ 78C1

Dunstaffnage Castle
- 5km (3 miles) north of Oban, off the A85
- ☎ 01631 562465
- 🕐 Apr–Sep, daily 9:30–6:30 (4:30 Oct–Mar)
- ✋ Cheap

The magnificent interior of historic Scone Palace

PERTH ✪✪

Once the capital of Scotland, Perth is now a prosperous market town in the heart of rich farmlands. Visit the Victorian water-driven oat mill at Lower City Mills and the cobbled streets around it. Bell's Cherrybank Gardens has the largest collection of heathers in Britain and a super children's play area, and at the Caithness Glass factory you can see glass blown in the traditional way.

Scone, a couple of miles north, where all the monarchs of Scotland were crowned on the Stone of Destiny, is the historic heart of Scotland. Ancient **Scone Palace** was restored and extended in the 19th century and this elegant, restrained, Gothic mansion is home to the Earl of Mansfield. The grounds, the house and the history are fascinating, but there is also an extraordinary collection of furniture, porcelain, delicate ivories, and papier mâché which once belonged to Louis XV of France.

✚ 79D1

Scone Palace
- Off the A93 Braemar Road, 3km (2 miles) northeast of Perth
- ☎ 01738 552300
- 🕐 Apr–Oct 9:30–5:30; last admission 4:45; grounds open until 5:45
- 🍴 Restaurant (££) and coffee shop (£)
- ✋ Moderate

79D2

Pass of Killiecrankie

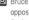 Off the A9, 5km (3 miles) north of Pitlochry

☎ 01796 473233

◷ Visitors' centre: Apr–Oct, daily 10–5:30 (Jul–Aug 9:30–6)

🍴 Snack bar (£)

👤 Cheap

✚ 79E1

British Golf Museum

✉ Bruce Embankment, opposite the Royal and Ancient Golf Club

☎ 01334 460046

◷ Easter to mid-Oct 9:30–5:30; winter Thu–Mon 11–3

👤 Moderate

Did this figure once ward off evil spirits at St Andrews Cathedral?

✚ 79D1

Stirling Castle

✉ Castle Wynd

☎ 01786 450000

👤 Apr–Sep, daily 9:30–6; Oct–Mar, daily 9:30–5

🍴 Tea room (£)

👤 Moderate

PITLOCHRY ⭐⭐

Pitlochry is a popular tourist centre on the banks of the River Tummel, where the Blair Athol Distillery has been making its famous malt since 1798. The power station produces electricity from the artificially created Loch Faskally, and the salmon ladder to help the fish negotiate the dam is a sight not to be missed. Pitlochry Festival Theatre is famous for its productions. Enjoy a backstage tour during the day and return in the evening for a performance of the latest play.

Near the town is the **Pass of Killiecrankie**, site of the famous Battle of Killicrankie in 1689 where the Jacobites, led by Graham of Claverhouse (Bonnie Dundee), defeated the government forces, although Dundee himself was killed. This deep wooded gorge has a visitors' centre with exhibits on the gorge and the battle.

ST ANDREWS ⭐⭐

Scotland's oldest university town is world famous as the home of golf, which has been played here since the 15th century. The Royal and Ancient Golf Club is the governing body of the sport and in 1873 the first British Open Championship was held here. The **British Golf Museum** is the best there is, with lots of hands-on stuff and plenty of history. However, if golf is not your scene take a walk around the historic streets to the great cathedral, once the largest in Scotland. It was consecrated in 1318 in the presence of King Robert the Bruce and destroyed in 1559 by supporters of John Knox. An impressive ruin, it is particularly beautiful at twilight in half silhouette.

STIRLING ⭐⭐⭐

Stirling Castle, like Edinburgh, is perched atop the plug of an extinct volcano, but in many ways Stirling is more dramatic. Surrounded by a wide plain, the castle is the most prominent sight for miles around and in past times the narrow bridge here was a strategic gateway between North and South. Many of the decisive battles in Scotland's history, including Stirling Bridge (1297) and Bannockburn (1314) were fought around here. At the

Lady's Rock in the cemetery there is a pointer to all the surrounding battle sites. Bannockburn's visitors' centre details the battle in an excellent audio-visual presentation. The Wallace Monument high on the cliffs overlooking the site of the Battle of Stirling Bridge contains the hero's massive two-handed sword.

THE TROSSACHS ✪✪✪

This wild countryside of moors, hills and forests, from Loch Katrine to Loch Lomond, was the haunt of Rob Roy MacGregor – outlaw, cattle thief, murderer or Scottish hero depending on your point of view. At any rate he died at a ripe old age in his own bed and is buried in the beautiful churchyard at Balquhidder. The Trossachs is the largest area of wilderness in central Scotland. There is excellent walking, climbing and fishing and the scenery is spectacular. If you can't make it to the Highlands, this is as near as you'll get to the majestic scale of the north. Its position right at the heart of Scotland means that it is easily accessible, but unfortunately, always crowded.

The two main towns in the area are Callander and Aberfoyle.

✚ 79D1

ℹ Argyll, the Isles, Loch Lomond, Stirling and Trossachs Tourist Board, Old Town Jail, St John's Street, Stirling ☎ 01786 445222; fax: 01786 471301

Loch Katrine in the heart of MacGregor country

The North

The Highlands and Islands are the Scotland of literature, romance and the movies, a vast area, much of it unforgiving mountain or natural moorland. Many species of wildlife which have disappeared elsewhere survive in the scarcely populated wildernesses here. Scattered ruined cottages remain, testimony to a more populous past before the Clearances in the 18th and 19th centuries, when the landlords drove the people from the land in favour of more profitable sheep.

Highlanders emigrated in droves to the New World, taking with them their oral traditions of music and storytelling and their memories of the land they left behind. Exiled Scots and their descendants get very nostalgic at the mention of misty glens, heather-covered hillsides and dark deep lochs. It is easy to mock, but travel this land once and you will understand how they feel.

' From the long shieling of the misty island, mountains divide us and a waste of seas. Yet still the blood is strong, the heart is Highland, and we in dreams behold The Hebrides. '

ANON

Aberdeen

Aberdeen, the grey granite city of the North, is the hub of Scotland's oil industry, a thriving fishing port and home to one of the four ancient universities of Scotland. Surprisingly, for the most northerly city of Scotland, it is famed for its imaginative and prolific gardens. The nightlife is lively on account of the university and the prosperity of its cosmopolitan population. Understanding the language, however, can present problems and a crash course in the Doric, the local dialect, might be a good idea. In the meantime, to the standard greeting of 'Fit like?', simply answer 'Nae bad, foo's yersel?' Translated it means 'How are you?', 'Not bad, how are you?'

What to See in Aberdeen

ABERDEEN MARITIME MUSEUM

The 1953 Provost Ross's house, one of the oldest buildings in the city, is home to this remarkable museum which tells the story of Aberdeen's maritime heritage. Everything is covered, from herring fishing and whaling to ship-building and the late 20th-century oil industry. The small ancient rooms combine with state-of-the-art computers, audio-visual technology, artefacts and oral history to bring the past to life.

79F3
Shiprow
01224 337700
Daily 10–5 (12–3 Sun)
Moderate

Ship's model and ancient figurehead in Aberdeen's Maritime Museum

FISH MARKET AND HARBOUR

Fishing is still one of the mainstays of the local economy and few sights can compare with the bustling harbour where fishing vessels lie alongside oil-rig supply boats and modern cruise liners. Pay an early morning visit to the fish market to mingle with the buyers and fishermen as thousands of tons of freshly landed fish are bid for then loaded into huge refrigerated trucks to be transported throughout the UK.

79F3

This unusual looking building was the former home of Provost Skene

79F3
✉ 45 Guestrow, off Broad Street
☎ 01224 641086
🕐 Mon–Sat 10–5, Sun 1–4
🍴 Provost Skene's Kitchen (£)
♿ Free

PROVOST SKENE'S HOUSE ⭐⭐

Dating from 1545, Aberdeen's oldest private dwelling house was the home of its provost (mayor), Sir George Skene, from 1676 to 1685, and is preserved almost unchanged. Astonishingly, its luminous religious paintings survived Reformation zeal to obliterate popish imagery and years of neglect. Finally, as a slum threatened with demolition, it was saved to become a museum in 1953. It provides a faithful representation of life for the comfortable burghers of Aberdeen in the late 17th century.

79F3
✉ The Tram Sheds, 170 Constitution Street
☎ 01224 640340
🕐 Mon–Sat 10–5, Sun 11:30–5
♿ Moderate

SATROSPHERE SCIENCE CENTRE ⭐⭐⭐

This is the only permanent interactive exhibition of Science and Technology in Scotland and a great place to take children. There are no 'DO NOT TOUCH' signs. The message is – do, touch, look, feel. About 80 of the 150 exhibits and experiments are on display at any one time. You can find out about the geological formation of northeast Scotland, marvel at the industry and organisation inside a beehive then compare it with a colony of ants, guess what the mystery sticky liquids are, test the speed of your reactions, experience the Satrosphere's very own black hole and much, much more. Fascinating for visitors of all ages, it may trigger a lifelong interest in science.

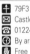
79F3
✉ Castle Street
☎ 01224 621167
🕐 By arrangement
♿ Free

TOLBOOTH MUSEUM ⭐⭐

The Tolbooth Museum, within the granite Town House, was the town gaol in 17th-century Aberdeen. The claustro-phobic narrow staircases and cramped cells chillingly evoke the grim existence of prisoners here. An audio-visual display and a lifelike model of a prisoner tell tales of the wretched life and of escapes from the bleak conditions.

What to See in the North

BALLATER AND BALMORAL ✪✪

Balmoral, a fine example of Scottish Baronial architecture, was converted to a private residence for Queen Victoria in 1855 and became a favourite summer residence for the Royal Family. The local shops in Ballater flaunt their 'By Royal Appointment' signs. The town is a grand base for exploring the area, and Balmoral Estate hires out ponies for pony trekking.

✚ 79E2
✉ Balmoral Estate: 13km (8 miles) west of Ballater on the A93
☎ 013397 42534
🕓 Mid-Apr to end Jul, daily 10–5. Closed Sun in Apr
🍴 Refreshments (£)
✋ Moderate

BETTYHILL ✪

The tiny coastal village of Bettyhill, at the centre of the local crofting community, suffered mass emigration during the Highland Clearances. The tiny **Strathnaver Museum**, in the former church, tells the story of some of the most horrific evictions, ordered by Elizabeth, Countess of Sutherland. Ironically the village was named after her. Near by are two of the whitest sand beaches in Britain and the Invernaver Nature Reserve, where otters and Arctic terns can often be spotted.

✚ 79D5

Strathnaver Museum
✉ In the old church
☎ 01641 521418
🕓 Apr–Oct, Mon–Sat 10–1, 2–5 (and by arrangement)
✋ Cheap

THE CAIRNGORMS ✪✪

Within the area of this range of mountains, outdoor enthusiasts can find skiing, canoeing, mountaineering, cycling and walking and a rich variety of flora and fauna. The 40km (25 miles) of the Lairig Ghru, running through a majestic mountain pass from Aviemore to Braemar, are reputed to be the best walk in Scotland, although its unpredictable weather and biting cold can test the endurance of the most experienced walker. However, there are lots of shorter, less demanding walks in this glorious landscape. Aviemore village is ideal for exploring the area and its numerous shops sell and rent equipment. Nearby Loch Morlich Watersports and the Scottish National Sports Council's Glenmore Lodge provide facilities and training.

✚ 79D3
ℹ Grampian Road, Aviemore
☎ 01479 810363
🕓 Mon–Sat 9–5, Sun 10–4

The majestic Cairngorms offer some of Scotland's finest walking

NORTHERN SCOTLAND

78C2

Clansmen's Centre

✉ On the banks of the canal
in Fort Augustus

☎ 01320 366444

🕐 Apr, May, Jun, Sep 11–5;
Jul, Aug 10–6

💷 Cheap

Above: *fishing boat
moored on the
Caledonian Canal*

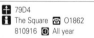 79D3

Cromarty Courthouse

✉ Church Street

☎ 01381 600418

🕐 Apr–Oct, daily 10–5; Nov,
Dec, Mar noon–4

💷 Moderate

 79D4

ℹ The Square ☎ 01862
810916 🕐 All year

Opposite: *the Dog Falls in
scenic Glen Affric*

CALEDONIAN CANAL AND THE GREAT GLEN

One of Thomas Telford's greatest engineering achieve-
ments was the Caledonian Canal linking lochs Ness, Oich,
Lochy and Linnhe from Inverness in the east to Fort
William in the west. A slow boat through the Great Glen,
watching the reflection of forest greenery or massed
broom along the banks is a tranquil and awesome
experience. For the more energetic there are lots of off-
road walking or cycling trails on disused military roads, the
old railway line or the towpath. At Fort Augustus, the
Clansmen's Centre illustrates 17th-century clan life in a
reconstructed turf house.

CROMARTY ⭐⭐

Cromarty is a picturesque village on the northeast coast of
the Black Isle. The local museum in the old **courthouse**
and the thatched cottage of Hugh Miller's birthplace
between them bring the varied past of this little port vividly
to life. You can take a boat trip to watch dolphins,
porpoises and even, on occasion, killer whales. However,
the massive oil rigs of Nigg and Invergordon cannot be
ignored, dominating the Cromarty Firth by day and lighting
up the night.

CULLODEN BATTLEFIELD (► 18, TOP TEN)

DORNOCH ⭐

In 1722 Dornoch was the last place in Scotland to burn a
witch. To the south of the town square, the Witch's Stone
is a reminder of the poor soul who was roasted in a barrel
of tar for allegedly turning her daughter into a pony. The
centre-piece of the square is the tiny cathedral, all but
destroyed in the 16th century and extensively rebuilt in the
19th century, incorporating skulls and coffins and other
intimations of mortality.

FORT GEORGE ✪

After the rout of Bonnie Prince Charlie's Highland army at Culloden in 1746, the Hanoverians embarked on a drastic plan for subduing 'rebellious Scots'. One measure was the construction of Fort George, on a spit running into the Moray Firth. It continues as an army barracks to this day and is the home of the **Regimental Museum of the Queen's Own Highlanders**. Allow half a day to visit. The walk along the ramparts is a mile.

GLEN AFFRIC ✪✪✪

As well as having some of the most serious walking, Glen Affric is undoubtedly one of the most beautiful glens in Scotland, with stretches of lovely lochs and forestry. The abundance of birch, pine and alder which grace the glen, is a glorious sight in blazing autumn colours. It has one of the most remote youth hostels in Britain, requiring a hike of several miles to reach it.

FORT WILLIAM

Fort William's location, at the foot of the Great Glen and with the bulk of Ben Nevis to the east, makes it a popular centre for walkers and mountaineers. It is also at the head of Loch Linnhe and it is here that you will find **Ocean Frontier**. The centrepiece 'Atlantic Reef Pool' is a 5-metre (16ft) deep underwater theatre where visitors can enjoy the experience of a deep sea dive in the safety of a totally controlled environment.

➕ 79D3
✉ B9039, off the A96 west of Nairn

Regimental Museum of the Queen's Own Highlanders
☎ 01667 462800 ext 8701
🕐 Apr–Sep, daily 10–6; winter, Mon–Fri 10–4
💷 Moderate

➕ 78C3
✉ Southwest of Cannich, off the A831

➕ 78C2

Ocean Frontier
✉ An Aird
☎ 01397 703786
🕐 Daily 10–6 (last entry 4:30)
💷 Moderate

GLEN COE (➤ 20–21, TOP TEN)

INVEREWE GARDENS 😊😊

The Gulf Stream flows around the west coast of Scotland producing a warm temperate climate, ideal for gardens. Inverewe was created between 1862 and 1922 by the estate owner, Osgood Mackenzie. The garden has spilled out from its original walled enclave to cover the peninsula. Scots pine, birch, oak and rowan stand alongside semi-tropical exotic plants in a series of delightful small gardens, interconnected by miles of paths.

🪧 78C4
✉ Poolewe
☎ 01445 781200
🕐 Daily 9:30–sunset
🍴 Restaurant (£)
✋ Moderate

*Shrubs and trees at
Inverewe Gardens*

🪧 79D3
ℹ Castle Wynd ☎ 01463
234353 🕐 All year

INVERNESS 😊😊

Inverness is an attractive town, built mainly in the 19th century, with a fine cathedral and castle. Situated on the Moray Firth at the eastern end of the Caledonian Canal, it is the largest town in the Highlands, an important transport hub and the best base for exploring the area.

🪧 78D2

Highland Folk Museum
✉ Duke Street
☎ 01540 661307
🕐 Mar–May and Sep–Oct,
Mon–Fri 10:30–4:30
(guided tours only);
Jun–Aug, Mon–Sat
10:30–5, Sun 1–5
✋ Moderate

KINGUSSIE 😊😊

Kingussie, a typical small town built round a single main street, is an oasis of tranquillity bypassed by the hurly-burly of the main artery north, the A9. At the **Highland Folk Museum** you can explore reconstructions of a Lewis black house (a traditional Hebridean low stone dwelling with thatched roof), a salmon smoking shed and a water mill, as well as finding out everything there is to know about the history of the area. Near by the ruins of Ruthven Barracks stand proud and roofless against the skyline. They were part of the fortifications built to ensure stability in the region after the Jacobite Rebellion of 1745. From Ruthven you can walk a surviving stretch of General Wade's military road, crossing a perfectly preserved example of a Wade bridge near Dalwhinnie.

Castle Urquhart, Loch Ness. The perfect location for a spot of monster hunting

LOCH NESS ✪✪✪

The world-famous loch is forever linked to its resident beastie, the Loch Ness Monster. The loch is long and deep and swarming with Nessie spotters. At Drumnadrochit there are two monster centres: the Original Loch Ness Monster Exhibition, and the considerably better **Official Loch Ness Exhibition Centre**.

Castle Urquhart, a couple of miles south, is the best monster spotting site, where most of the Nessie photographs have been taken. The ruins of the 14th-century castle themselves are worth a visit. Perched atop a rocky cliff the castle was of strategic importance in guarding the Great Glen. It was destroyed in 1692 to prevent its use by the Jacobites.

➕ 79D3

Official Loch Ness Exhibition Centre
✉ Drumnadrochit
☎ 01456 450573
🕐 Daily Nov–Mar 10–4; Easter–May and Oct 9:30–5:30; Jun and Sep 9:30–6:30; Jul and Aug 9–8:30
💷 Expensive

ROTHIEMURCHUS ✪

The huge estate of Rothiemurchus, belonging to the Grant family, extends from the village of Aviemore to the Cairngorm plateaux. The lovely woodlands here, with the Cairngorms forming a backdrop, are particularly noted for their magnificent Caledonian pine. From the estate visitors' centre, there's access to a superb mountain bike track and miles of footpaths through forests, over heather moorlands and by lochs and rivers. There is also a nature trail around Loch an Eilean and other activities include clay-pigeon shooting, ranger walks and fishing on the Spey.

➕ 79D3
✉ 1.5km (1 mile) southeast from Aviemore on the Ski Road
☎ 01479 810858
🕐 Daily 9:30–5:30
💷 Free

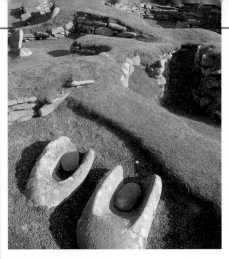

Jarlshof, Shetland's prehistoric settlement

Shetland & Orkney

These islands were formerly Norwegian, and the Norse influence is still evident in language and customs. Orkney is a few miles off the Scottish mainland, while Shetland is 96km (60 miles) further north. Each one is a scattering of islands, abounding in wildlife, particularly sea birds. In both, the Mainland refers to the main island while the rest of Scotland is known as 'The Sooth'.

29D4, 29C4

> ### DID YOU KNOW?
> The islanders of Foula still use the ancient Julian calendar. Initially this was because the island was remote but nowadays they just like to be different. However, they switch to the standard calendar when it suits them, such as New Year, which they can celebrate on two separate dates.

What to See in Shetland

FOULA ✪✪
About 22km (14 miles) east of the Mainland is Foula, a world apart. Traces of an ancient way of life – peat fires and eking out a subsistence living – cling to this remote island. Until a few years ago, the island schoolteacher was responsible for christenings, marriages and funerals in his role as Church of Scotland missionary. Foula teems with bird life, particularly puffins and great skuas.

29D4
Ferries to Foula from Walls ☎ 01595 753226 for information

JARLSHOF ✪✪
This ancient settlement was inhabited from the Stone Age to the 17th century. There's a broch (round tower made of two layers of stones with stairs built into the thickness of the wall) and a medieval building, but the most interesting dwellings are the Norse longhouses and the complex wheelhouse structures with underground corridors, bedrooms and central hearths.

29D4
✉ Sumburgh
☎ 01950 460112
🕐 Apr–Sep, daily 9:30–6:30.
👣 Cheap

LERWICK ✪✪

Lerwick has an attractive harbour where fishing boats jostle for space alongside transporters for the oil industry and the Greenpeace *Rainbow Warrior*, a frequent visitor. The narrow winding main street runs behind the harbour front and countless tiny alleys climb steeply up the hill.

Up Helly Aa, once a pagan fire festival to celebrate the end of the ancient Yule celebration, is now a well organised spectacle in which a thousand men with blazing torches march through the streets of Lerwick. Behind them they drag a Viking galley to the burning ground where they throw their torches into the vessel. If you can't be there to see it in January there is an excellent exhibition with an audio-visual with examples of Viking costumes and pictures of bearded warriors in winged helmets, standing before the burning craft.

What to See in Orkney

ITALIAN CHAPEL ✪✪✪

Although built from Nissen huts, concrete, barbed wire and paint by Italian POWs in 1943, the love and reverence which went into this exquisite little gem are evident. Artist Domenico Chiocchetti designed the interior, creating *trompe-l'oeil* stonework and windows, and a magnificent fresco altarpiece.

KIRKWALL AND ST MAGNUS CATHEDRAL ✪✪✪

Kirkwall is the largest town in Orkney and the island capital. St Magnus Cathedral, founded by Jarl Rognvlad in 1137 and built over a period of 300 years, has architectural details ranging from Norman to early Gothic. The exquisite carving, the glowing red and yellow stone and its small size give it a strange feeling of delicacy and lightness for a medieval cathedral.

MAES HOWE ✪✪✪

This neolithic burial chamber is the finest chambered tomb in Western Europe. You have to creep through a long narrow stone tunnel to reach the central chamber. It was built 4,000 years ago with such precision that the sun lights the tunnel at sunset on midwinter. When opened last century, no treasures were found. Vikings had beaten the Victorians to the plunder, leaving a collection of Runic graffiti which would translate well to lavatory walls today.

SKARA BRAE (► 24, TOP TEN)

➕ 29D4

Up Helly Aa
✉ Galley Shed, off Sunniva Street
🕓 Mid-May to mid-Sep, Tue 2–4, 7–9, Fri 5–9, Sat 2–4
ℹ Shetland Island Tourism, Market Cross ☎ 01595 693434
✋ Cheap

➕ 29C4
✉ Lamb Holm
🕓 Apr–Sep 9AM–10PM; winter 9–4:30
✋ Free

➕ 29C4
ℹ Orkney Tourist Board, 6 Broad Street, Klrkwall ☎ 01856 872856

Above: *a lifeboat in Lerwick harbour*

➕ 29C4
✉ Stenness
☎ 01856 761606
🕓 Apr–Sep, daily 9:30–6:30; Oct–Mar, Mon–Sat 9:30–4:30, Sun 2–4:30
🍴 Café (£)
✋ Cheap

Shetland, Mousa Island and Broch

Distance
6km (4 miles)

Time
3 hours (including ferry)

Start/end point
The pier at Leebitton Harbour, Sandwick
✠ 29D4

Lunch
There are no facilities on Mousa, so take a packed lunch

Mousa Broch, an ancient Pictish fortification

Mousa is a small, uninhabited island to the east of Mainland Shetland, with an unrivalled example of a broch – the circular, fortified, drystone tower of the Iron Age. Abundant wildlife includes seals and storm petrels, eider ducks, waders and skuas, which swoop and dive everywhere, unmoved by the approach of humans.

Turn right from the jetty and follow the path along the coast to your right until you come to the broch.

Built between 100 BC and AD 100, Mousa Broch, featured in the great Viking Sagas, remains almost intact. A narrow passage leads to an inner courtyard where the encircling massive stone wall bears in on you as you look up at the circle of sky 12m above. Torches are supplied to climb the narrow, worn stairs in the dark space within the walls. At the top you can see where great beams would have supported the turf roof and view a coastline that the original builders would still recognise.

Follow the path round the coast from the broch or head inland with the remains of a house on your right.

The map you get from the boatman indicates areas to be avoided during the nesting season. Either way you will reach two sheltered bays on the east side where seals gather. There may be just two or three swimming or possibly a hundred or so in and out of the water.

From the bay follow the path back to the jetty and the small stone cottage that now serves as a shepherd's bothy.

Skye & the Western Isles

This group of islands contain some of the bleakest and most beautiful scenery in Scotland. From the majestic Cuillins of Skye through the flat water-logged moors of North Uist and the rolling hills of Harris to the timeless charm of the smaller islands, Eigg, Muck, Rum, Canna, Barra and Eriskay, you could spend a lifetime exploring here. Walk the ancient paths and hill tracks, seek out secluded bays or visit prehistoric settlements and still there are further delights to uncover.

What to See in Skye & the Western Isles

CALLANISH STONES, ISLE OF LEWIS ✪✪✪

Built over 4,000 years ago, and 1,000 years before the pyramids of Egypt, this is possibly the most spectacular and intact prehistoric site in Europe. Standing on a raised site overlooking Loch Roag, the 4.5m-high stones form the shape of a Celtic cross. The main part of the site is a circle of 13 stones with an avenue of 19 monoliths leading north.

ℹ️ Western Isles Tourist Board, 26 Cromwell Street, Stornoway, Isle of Lewis ☎ 01851 703088

✚ 78B4
✉ Callanish
☎ 01851 621422
🕐 Apr–Sep, daily 10–6 (closes at 4 in winter)
🍴 Café (£)
💷 Cheap

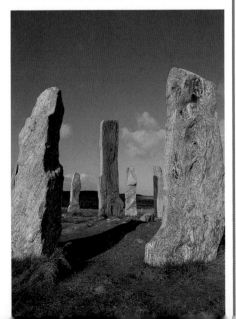

The standing stones of Callanish. Once a place of worship or perhaps a prehistoric calendar?

78B4
✉ Old Grainstore, Bayhead Street
☎ 01851 704500
🕐 Apr–Dec, Mon–Sat 9–6
Cheap

Skye's Cuillin mountains beyond the old bridge at Sligachan

LEWIS LOOM CENTRE, ISLE OF LEWIS ✪✪

Harris tweed production is one of the mainstays of the local economy in the Outer Hebrides and is still woven by hand. The only place in the islands where the entire production process can be seen is the Lewis Loom Centre in Stornoway, where Ronnie Mackenzie has set up a small museum and exhibition centre. Ronnie will demonstrate carding, spinning and warping, and explain about natural and synthetic dyes. Then he'll weave some cloth, talk about waulking the finished material and answer questions. His shop stocks a wide variety of Harris tweed clothing.

78B3
✉ Inverarish
☎ 01478 660266
🕐 Accommodation all year, activities Mar–Oct
Expensive

RAASAY OUTDOOR CENTRE, RAASAY ✪✪

Raasay is the place for anyone looking for an adventure sport holiday. The centre provides equipment and instruction for a bewildering array of activities including sailing, water-skiing, sailboarding, mountain biking, walking and climbing. Accommodation is provided in the house where Dr Samuel Johnstone (1709–84), a leading journalist and literary figure, and his biographer, James Boswell (1704–95), lodged during their tour of the Hebrides. The activities are open to day visitors, too.

78B3
✉ Near Loch Ainort
☎ 01470 552206
🕐 Apr–Oct, Mon–Sat 9:30–5:30
🍴 Tea machine
Cheap

SKYE MUSEUM OF ISLAND LIFE, ISLE OF SKYE ✪✪✪

This 'living museum' is a series of seven thatched black houses, reconstructed to form an ancient island township. The original black house on the site is much as it was when it was last inhabited in the late 1950s. Here locals re-create the crofting way of life as it was a century ago. Behind the museum is the grave of Flora MacDonald who helped Bonnie Prince Charlie to escape the Hanoverian forces after his defeat at Culloden.

Harris & Lewis

This coastal drive round the islands of Lewis and Harris takes in the most important attractions in the Hebrides.

From Stornoway take the A859 towards Tarbert which is 56km (35 mile) away on Harris. Continue on the A859 to Leverburgh. From Leverburgh continue on the A859 as far as Rodel, then follow the local road as it meanders along the east coast via Manish to rejoin the A859 south of Tarbert.

Called the Golden Highway, because of the expense of building it, this is a winding, single track road with passing places. It connects a number of small remote settlements strung out across a land which resembles a moonscape – rugged, rocky, empty and painfully beautiful.

From Tarbert drive back towards Stornoway on the A859. At Leurbost, turn left on the local road which links with the A858 at Achmore. Follow this road to Callanish.

The standing stones of Callanish (► 87), constructed about a thousand years before the pyramids, stand above Loch Roag.

Continue on the road past Carloway, Arnol and through Barvas to Lional, then follow the signs for the Butt of Lewis.

Greosabhagh	$1^1\!/_2$
(Scadabhagh	4)
Collam	$2^1\!/_2$
Cliuthar	3
Stocinis	4
Leac a Li	5

Carloway Broch is worth a visit, and the nearby village of Garenin with its restored black houses should not be missed. Arnol Black House was built in 1885 and served continuously as a dwelling until 1964. The young woman who lived there with her mother is now the caretaker/guide.

From the lighthouse at the Butt of Lewis return by the same route as far as Barvas then turn left on to the A857 to Stornoway.

Distance
298km (185 miles)

Time
6–8 hours depending on stops

Start/end point
Stornoway
✚ 28A4

Lunch
Harris Hotel, Tarbert (££)
☎ 01859 502154

Road signs in the Western Isles are in Gaelic

89

✚ 78 C4

ℹ Argyle Street ☎ 01854
612135 ⏰ Easter–Nov,
Mon–Fri 9–6, Sun 1–6

**Leckmelm Shrubbery and
Arboretum**

✉ 5km (3 miles) south of
Ullapool on A835

☎ 0131 229 1870 (Scottish
Gardens Scheme)

⏱ May–Sep 10–6

💷 Cheap

*The tiny houses of
Ullapool stretch out along
the shores of Loch Broom*

ULLAPOOL ★★

Ullapool, at the head of Loch Broom, was built as a planned fishing village in 1788 by the British Fisheries Society. Today, it is still a bustling fishing port, as well as the ferry terminal for the Western Isles and the main base for exploring Wester Ross. It has a lively cultural centre at the Ceilidh Place (➤ 38), where people can enjoy the outdoors by day and sample live traditional music and dancing in the evening. The surrounding countryside abounds in walks such as the old drove road to Loch Achall and back over the summit of Meall Mor, with a breathtaking view over Loch Broom and the Summer Isles.

The Isles are a small group of uninhabited islands accessible by boat from Ullapool and Achiltibuie during the summer months. Most trips allow an hour on shore on Tanera Mhor, the largest island in the group. As well as sea birds, you are likely to see seals, dolphins and porpoises. Five kilometres (3 miles) from Ullapool on Loch Broom, you will find **Leckmelm Shrubbery and Arboretum**, dating from the 1870s, which is renowned for its rare trees and plants, including rhododendrons and azaleas.

Corrieshalloch Gorge, on the A835 south of Ullapool, is a 1.5km- (1-mile) long, 60m-deep box canyon with an information board which tells you all about its geological and botanical interest. However, it's the Falls of Measach that most people come to see. The 45m cascade can be viewed from a narrow suspension bridge that spans the gorge or from the observation platform.

Where To...

Eat and Drink	92–9
Stay	100–105
Shop	106–109
Take the Children	110–11
Be Entertained	112–16

Above: *the flags of Scotland – the Lion Rampant and the Saltire*
Right: *this fish design is on a window in the Scottish Fisheries Museum at Anstruther*

Edinburgh & the Borders

Prices

Approximate prices for a three-course meal, excluding wine, for one person are shown by the £ symbol:

£   = under £15
££   = £15–25
£££ = over £25

Edinburgh

Atrium (£££)

Mediterranean meets Midlothian is one way to describe the menu here. Try the venison in cherry sauce with cabbage and bacon, and seared scallops as a starter.

✉ **Cambridge Street** ☎ **0131 228 8882**

Bene Fish & Chips (£)

Situated on the historic Royal Mile, this family run take-away fish and chip shop is among the finest in the capital. Bene also makes great pizzas.

✉ **162 Canongate** ☎ **0131 557 1092**

Caledonian Hotel (£–£££)

Chisholms restaurant serves brasserie-style food all day. Particularly popular is their haggis, neeps and tatties which you can have as a starter or main course. Following extensive refurbishment The Pompadour restaurant has re-established itself as one of the premier eating places in the capital.

✉ **Princes Street** ☎ **0131 222 8888**

Channings Hotel (££)

A blend of Scottish and European cooking, a feature of many Edinburgh restaurants, is the speciality of Channings Restaurant. Try, in particular, the freshly baked bread and the scallops and spring onions.

✉ **South Learmonth Gardens** ☎ **0131 315 2226**

George Inter-Continental (£££)

Le Chambertin is an intimate French restuarant where the quality of the food is matched by the enthusiasm of the staff. Ask for a window seat looking out on to the Georgian New Town and let the sommelier recommend a wine.

✉ **19–21 George Street** ☎ **0131 225 1251**

Sheraton Grand (£££)

Classic French and Scottish cuisine. Particularly good for seafood such as salmon, scallops and roast sea bass. The wine list has got to be seen to be believed.

✉ **1 Festival Square** ☎ **0131 229 9131**

Winter Glen (££)

Blair Glen and Graham Winter's magic basement restaurant where Graham produces great Scottish cooking and a very wicked warm chocolate cake.

✉ **3A1 Dundas Street** ☎ **0131 477 7060**

The Witchery and Secret Garden (££)

This is the best eating experience in Edinburgh. The light, airy Secret Garden with its tapestry-hung stone walls downstairs and the atmospheric, candle-lit, Witchery, combine with the best in Scottish cuisine and desserts to die for.

✉ **352 Castle Hill, Royal Mile** ☎ **0131 225 5613**

The Borders

Biggar

Shieldhill Castle (££)

Daily changing menu which features delights such as chicken, spinach and tomato roulade with herb salad and walnut oil.

✉ **Quothquan** ☎ **01899 220035**

Chirnside
Chirnside Hall (££)
The dining-room has grand views over the surrounding countryside and offers seasonal dishes such as poached monkfish served with a tartlet of langoustine and crisp-edged duckling with a honey and soy sauce, prepared from quality Scottish produce.

✉ **On the A6105 Berwick-upon-Tweed/Duns road**
☎ **01890 818219**

Gullane
Greywalls Hotel (£££)
Set four-course dinner in a dining-room overlooking Muirfield golf course, serving Aberdeen Angus beef, Loch Fyne smoked salmon and local lamb and cheeses. The ideal place to treat yourself.

✉ **Muirfield** ☎ **01620 842144**

La Potinière (££)
Very popular and needs to be booked well in advance, but well worth the effort.

✉ **Main Street** ☎ **01620 843214** 🕐 **Lunch and dinner Wed–Sun**

Kelso
Roxburgh Hotel & Golf Course (££)
This is the Duke of Roxburgh's place and very popular with the huntin', fishin' and shootin' set. The Duke's estate supplies the Tweed salmon and wild game featured on the menu.

✉ **Heiton (5km/3 miles southwest of Kelso on the A698)**
☎ **01573 450331**

Kirknewton
Marriot Dalmahoy Hotel (££)
A plush place where guests are expected to wear a jacket and tie. The Pentland Restaurant overlooks the 18th hole of the golf course. Very good food as well.

✉ **On the A71, 3km (2 miles) east of Kirknewton** ☎ **0131 333 1845**

Linlithgow
Champany Inn (£££, lunch, ££)
An old mill house dating from the time of Mary, Queen of Scots, and with a long-standing reputation for quality Scottish dishes.

✉ **3km (2 miles) northeast** ☎ **01506 834532**

Melrose
Burt's Hotel (££)
Burt's, famous for its beef obtained from quality-assured farms, is a member of the Scotch Beef Club. The modern menu also features dishes such as chicken and sausage haggis and a lasagne of salmon and halibut served with ratatouille.

✉ **Market Square** ☎ **01896 822285**

Peebles
Cringletie House Hotel (£££)
Regional produce used extensively in an imaginative way to produce such delights as courgette and rosemary soup with crème fraiche.

✉ **3km (2 miles) north on the A703** ☎ **01721 730233**

Swinton
Wheatsheaf Hotel (££)
Small hotel on the village green. The menu features wood pigeon, duck and corn-fed chicken.

✉ **Main Street** ☎ **01890 860257**

Stovies
This is surely the food of the gods. Originally the poor person's stew made with very little meat and a lot of potatoes and vegetables, the recipe and contents vary by locality and preference. Nowadays you'll find it on the menus of some pubs and in snack bars. Carriers Quarters, 42 Bernard Street, Leith ☎ 0131 554 4122, one of Leith's oldest unaltered pubs, serves some of the best.

Glasgow & the Southwest

Deep Fried Mars Bars
This rather dubious Scottish delicacy is on sale in fish and chip shops throughout the land. Take one Mars bar, cover with batter, deep fry in hot oil for a few minutes then serve with chips. Tasty it is. Healthy it is not, and it's little wonder that Glasgow is the heart attack capital of Europe with this one on the menu.

Glasgow

Buttery Restaurant (£££)
More of an experience than a restaurant. Underneath the Kingston Bridge, this former corner pub has survived intact amid new housing. Step through the door into this remnant of old world elegance and sample some of the finest cooking in Scotland. Try breast of duckling soaked in champagne, whisky and honey followed by Perthshire lamb pressed between potato layers and conclude with iced fudge and marshmallow parfait.
✉ 652 Argyle Street ☎ 0141 221 8188

Glasgow Hilton (£££)
Several restaurants in the Glasgow Hilton, including Camerons, serve prime Scottish food and a wine list that can cater to the most discerning of palates.
✉ 1 Williams Street ☎ 0141 204 5555

Glasgow Moat House (££)
Another large city-centre hotel with several choices of restaurant serving informal meals to fine dining. The seafood is very tasty.
✉ Congress Road ☎ 0141 306 9988

Killermont Polo Club (££)
In a city with many Indian restaurants the Killermont Polo Club offers consistent quality coupled with friendly service.
✉ 2002 Maryhill Road, Maryhill Park ☎ 0141 946 5412

Nairns (££)
Celebrity chef Nick Nairn's place situated in a smart town house providing top-notch food at affordable prices. The set-price menu is very good value.
✉ 13 Woodside Crescent ☎ 0141 353 0707

La Parmigiana (££)
Locals, who should know a good deal, have supported this trattoria for years. The baked sea bass with a lemon butter sauce is tasty, as are the classic Italian dishes.
✉ 447 Great Western Road ☎ 0141 334 0686

Ubiquitous Chip (£–££)
Wonderful, popular restaurant and bistro near the University. The Scottish menu is served in the verdant courtyard restaurant or in the upstairs balcony.
✉ 12 Ashton Lane, Hillhead ☎ 0141 334 5007

Yes (£££)
Light, pleasant, downstairs restaurant serving delightfully prepared Scottish food. Particularly good is the Buccleuch beef, and the freshly baked bread with olive oil is for those of us who don't care about calories. Vegetarians are very well catered for here.
✉ 22 West Nile Street ☎ 0141 248 7878

The Southwest

Ayr

Fairfield House Hotel (££)
Timbale of smoked salmon filled with a lobster and sweet red pepper bavarois, and roast monkfish tails on a parsnip and potato cake with fresh pesto are just two of the mouth-watering seafood dishes on the menu.
✉ 12 Fairfield Road ☎ 01292 267461

Fouters Bistro (£–££)
Laurie and Fran Black have been at Fouters for 30 years. His interpretation of modern Scottish cooking makes this restaurant one of the most popular eating places in the west of Scotland.

✉ **2A Academy Street**
☎ **01292 261391**

Gatehouse of Fleet
Cally Palace Hotel (£££)
Simple and honest is how this grand hotel describes its dishes. Good Scottish fare based on local produce and prepared to the highest standard.

✉ **1.5km (1 mile) from Gatehouse** ☎ **01557 814341**

Girvan
Tasty Bites (£)
This main street café/restaurant is part of the Westcliffe Hotel Group, a family-run concern specialising in well-cooked tasty snacks and meals at affordable prices.

✉ **92 Dalrymple Street**
☎ **014657 15222**

Moffat
Beechwood Country House Hotel (££)
Pleasant wooded surroundings and a Victorian house provide the ambience in which to enjoy a regularly changing menu in a non-smoking dining-room.

✉ **Harthorpe Place** ☎ **01683 220210**

Moniaive
Craigdarroch Arms (£)
This very old, family-run hotel has an awesome reputation for the quality of its food. Ranging from inexpensive bar snacks, served by a blazing log fire in the lounge, to a full restaurant menu with such delights as pan-seared ostrich steaks and the famed Craigdarroch mixed grill.

✉ **High Street** ☎ **01848 200205**

Newton Stewart
Kirroughtree House (£££)
Duck with potatoes, celeriac purée, black pudding and ratatouille may sound like a terrible mixture but wait till you see how they are combined to create one of the mouth-watering dishes the hotel is famous for.

✉ **Minnigaff** ☎ **01671 402141**

Portpatrick
Knockinaam Lodge Hotel (£££)
Gourmet meals prepared from fresh local ingredients are served in a Victorian hunting lodge facing the Irish Sea.

✉ **East of Portpatrick off the A77** ☎ **01776 810471**

Troon
Highgrove House (£££)
Sitting on a hillside with stupendous views over the Firth of Clyde is one of the plus points of Highgrove House. Scottish cuisine using produce from all over the country, prepared in an imaginative and innovative manner is another.

✉ **Old Loans Road** ☎ **01292 312511**

Turnberry
Westin Turnberry Hotel (£££)
If you can't afford to stay at the hotel at the very least treat yourself to a meal here, or perhaps afternoon tea.

✉ **Just north of the village on the A719** ☎ **01655 331000**

Square Slice
Made from ground meat, breadcrumbs and spice, this excellent sausage, peculiar to Scotland, is formed into a long square loaf and cut into slices. Its proper name is Lorne Sausage, but no one calls it that. Try it fried for breakfast or in a bun or sandwich with an optional topping of a fried egg and fried tattie (potato) scone.

Central Scotland

Selkirk Bannocks

Although this mouth-watering cake can be bought throughout Scotland, the best ones will be found in the Scottish Borders. They're large, flat, round loaves made by adding butter, sugar and fruit to bread dough. Then they're baked on a gridle or in the oven. Look for the ones made from the original recipe.

Anstruther
Cellar Restaurant (££)
This used to be a cooperage where barrels were made for the herring industry. Now herrings are served to the customers along with a wide variety of other fare, East Neuk crab and meat.

✉ **24 East Green** ☎ **01333 310378**

Arduaine
Loch Melfort Hotel (£££)
Sit in the dining-room gazing out over Loch Melfort to the Sound of Jura and you'll forget all about food. Until it arrives that is. Splendid, mouth-watering fare based on local seafood. Be sure to try the disgustingly decadent bread-and-butter pudding.

✉ **On the A816 midway between Oban and Lochgilphead** ☎ **01852 200233**

Auchterarder
The Gleneagles Hotel (£££)
One of Scotland's finest hotels offering some of the country's finest cooking. Soufflé created from Lanark blue cheese and pine nuts, chargrilled quail and smoked venison are just a few of the dishes guaranteed to get the juices flowing.

✉ **On A823** ☎ **01764 662231**

Balloch
De Vere Cameron House Hotel (££–£££)
Sitting on the Bonnie Banks of Loch Lomond looking out on to Inchmurrin island and Ben Lomond, this hotel offers a choice of three restaurants, including the bar-diner in the nearby marina or the fine Georgian Room in the hotel.

✉ **Loch Lomond** ☎ **01389 755565**

Balquhidder
Monachyle Mhor (££)
Right in the heart of Rob Roy country and the romantic Braes of Balquhidder, the dining-room overlooks two lochs. Tom Lewis is a chef/proprietor who really understands food and how it should be cooked.

✉ **Off the A84, south of Lochearnhead** ☎ **01877 384622**

Killiecrankie
Killiecrankie House Hotel (££)
Pudding wines by the glass are a perfect reason for dining here. Or choose from the dessert list – the white chocolate delice is superb, as is the glazed lemon tart.

✉ **Take A9 north of Pitlochry, left on to B8019 before Killiecrankie** ☎ **01796 473220**

Lundin Links
Old Manor Hotel (££)
Modern British cooking, such as sautéed chicken livers with walnut mayonnaise and croutons, is served here.

✉ **Leven Road** ☎ **01333 320368**

Oban
Manor House Hotel (££)
Daily changing set menu is very much 'Auld Alliance' fare with Scottish ingredients getting the French treatment.

✉ **Gallanach Road** ☎ **01631 562087**

Peat Inn
Peat Inn (£££)
David Wilson has made the Peat Inn a watchword for superb cuisine locally and much further afield. Standing at the crossroads of a small hamlet not far from St

Andrews it is *the* place to eat in Fife.

 10km (6 miles) southwest of St Andrews at junction of the B940/B941 ☎ **01334 840206**

Perth

Huntingtower Hotel (££)

Reasonable fixed-price menu including creations such as a warm salad of seared scallops and rack of lamb with rosemary and mustard crust are served in the panelled restaurant of a country house hotel.

✉ **Crieff Road, Almondbank** ☎ **01738 583771**

Kinfauns Castle (£££)

Early 17th-century castle with late 20th-century, award-winning chef makes this one of the most sought-after restaurants in the country. The Scottish Gourmet Evenings rank as essential eating.

✉ **Kinfauns** ☎ **01738 620777**

Beppe Vittorio (££)

Superb Italian fare served by friendly staff in this wonderful restaurant.

✉ **181 South Street** ☎ **01738 628555**

Pitlochry

Knockendarroch House Hotel (££)

Victorian mansion looking over the Tummel Valley offers a set menu with two choices for each course. Try the fish in beer batter sauce and the rhubarb crumble.

✉ **Higher Oakfield** ☎ **01796 473473**

St Andrews

The Old Course Hotel (£££)

Dine well while looking out over the famous Old Course. Caesar salad, crispy Cajun onion rings and red fish with *bok choi* sit comfortably on the menu with Scottish beef and fish.

✉ **40 The Scores** ☎ **01334 474371**

Rufflets Country House (££)

The Garden Restaurant in this turreted mansion is an absolute pleasure. Local ingredients are combined with imagination to produce such delights as Brie baked with prosciutto in oatmeal, white grilled collops of Rannoch venison in a port and pickled walnut jus and an exquisite chocolate parfait with a delicate balance of flavours with crème anglaise and coffee. There is a great wine list, too, with seven sold by the glass.

✉ **Strathkinness Low Road** ☎ **01334 472594**

Stirling

Royal Hotel (££)

This Victorian hotel features a stylish restaurant serving such gems as haggis-stuffed chicken with a Drambuie sauce, scallops with saffron butter, followed by chocolate marquise with caramel sauce. The Sunday lunches are grand.

✉ **Henderson Street, Bridge of Allan** ☎ **01786 832284**

Taynuilt

Taychreggan Hotel (£££)

Once this was a drovers' inn on the north shore of Loch Awe, now it serves great Scottish food in a fixed-price, three-course menu with at least three choices of main course.

✉ **From the A85 take the B845 at Taynuilt to Kilchrenan and Taychreggan** ☎ **01866 833211**

High Tea

Once ubiquitous, this distinctly Scottish meal has fallen from fashion but can still be found in some old family-run hotels and restaurants. Typically it consists of bread and butter and an old-fashioned three-tiered cake stand piled high with scones, pancakes, shortbread and dreadfully fattening cakes, all washed down with copious quantities of tea.

The North

Forfar Bridies

Forfar is the home of the Bridie, a meat-filled flaky pastry delicacy which can be purchased from most Scottish bakers. Avoid the supermarket varieties. They vary in texture and quality but if you want to experience the genuine article seek out one of the Forfar bakers who still make them – huge, meaty and very tasty.

Aberdeen

Ardoe House (£££)

Five-course gourmet dinners are the speciality of the house, served in the wood-panelled splendour of a baronial mansion.
✉ **South Deeside Road, Blairs**
☎ **01224 867355**

Simpson's Hotel (££)

Opulent splendour where East meets East Coast. Moroccan columns support a colonnade of arches, flanking a palm court, complete with fountain, leading to a sweeping staircase. The food's 'nae bad' as well with Scottish ingredients such as black pudding and scallops given the Mediterranean treatment.
✉ **59 Queens Road** ☎ **01224 327777**

Ballater

Balgonie House Hotel (£££)

Crêpes Suzette, Scottish cheeses and meat on garlic potatoes form a small part of the eclectic menu in this fine Edwardian house. Superb bread as well.
✉ **Braemar Place** ☎ **013397 55482**

Green Inn (££)

An innovative selection of Scottish dishes with cosmopolitan flavours. Try the Scotch beef and Yorkshire pudding, and the iced Cranachan mousse.
✉ **9 Victoria Road** ☎ **01339 755701**

Dufftown

Taste of Speyside (£)

An absolute cracker. Cullen skink is on the menu, traditional clootie dumpling (▶ side panel), topped with Glenfiddich liquer and a host of local specialities including smoked venison. Finish with a glass of malt bearing the same name as the street.
✉ **10 Balvenie Street**
☎ **01340 820860**

Fort William

Crannog Restaurant (££)

Converted from an old fisherman's gear shed, this restaurant sits out on the pier. Naturally they serve seafood, mostly local.
✉ **Town Pier** ☎ **01397 705589**

Glamis

Castleton House Hotel (££)

Country house with 700-year-old moat. Try the fine whisky fruit tart, preceded perhaps by langoustine cappuccino followed by cod and crab fishcake on a dressing of mixed beans. Main dishes could be fillet of Scotch Beef with buttered spinach, dauphinoise potatoes and a red wine sauce.
✉ **Forfar** ☎ **01307 840340**

Inverness

Café 1 (£)

French bistro classics meet contemporary British. Try liver and bacon with an onion marmalade and potatoes and parsnip mash followed by a selection of French and Scottish cheeses all washed down with a glass or three of wine.
✉ **76 Castle Street** ☎ **01463 226200**

Kingussie

The Cross (£££)

Katie and David Young are the friendly proprietors of this former tweed mill, now a restaurant with accommodation. Bedrooms combine high quality with a light and airy touch, and similarly in the restaurant fresh local and seasonal produce is cooked in a deceptively simple manner and served caringly but with the minimum of fuss. Award-winning wine list.

✉ **Tweed Mill Brae, Ardbroilach Road** ☎ 01540 661166; e-mail relax@thecross.co.uk

Muir of Ord
The Dower House (££)
The fixed-price dinner is a bargain and the wines are reasonably priced in this small and intimate dining-room, but being close to Inverness and very popular, advance booking is essential.

✉ **Highfield** ☎ 01463 870090

Onich
Allt-nan-Ros Hotel (£££)
Fixed-price dinner menu full of tasty Scottish ingredients, on the shores of Loch Linnhe looking over to the Morven hills. Mine host wears his kilt, and the waitresses wear long tartan skirts.

✉ **Fort William** ☎ 01855 821210

Plockton
Haven Hotel (££)
Deep in the heart of Hamish Macbeth country, the Haven is in the village, which is the location for the popular TV series. The Haven uses the finest local produce including seafood, salmon, Scottish beef, venison and lamb

✉ **Innes Street** ☎ 01599 544223

Portree, Isle of Skye
Cuillin Hills Hotel (££)
Spectacular views of the Cuillins over Portree Bay are the highlight of an evening here. Built in 1870 as a hunting lodge for the Lord of the Isles, it is now one of the premier eating places on Skye. Specialities may include venison steak with juniper berry, gin and garlic *jus*, and oven-roasted pheasant with a green peppercorn whisky sauce.

✉ **Just north of Portree off the A855** ☎ 01478 612003

Shieldaig
Tigh an Eilean Hotel (££)
Scotland is full of splendid restaurants. This one is a corker. The cooking is simple and uses fresh, quality produce. Try the crab dijonnaise, grilled lamb cutlets or poached salmon hollandaise.

✉ **Off the A896** ☎ 01520 755251

Torridon
Loch Torridon Hotel (£££)
In the past the aristocracy captured all the great locations for castles, mansions and hunting lodges. This one, overlooking the excruciatingly beautiful Loch Torridon, is no exception. Try the lobster with cucumber spaghetti in a lobster and sherry sauce, or deer fillet with juniper and sweated red onions.

✉ **Off the A896, southwest of Kinlochewe** ☎ 01445 791242

Ullapool
The Ceilidh Palace (££)
This is the cultural centre of the northwest and among other attributes serves some of the finest cuisine to be found north of Inverness.

✉ **West Argyll Street** ☎ 01854 612103

Clootie Dumpling
The clootie dumpling is like a huge cake created by mixing flour, butter, dried fruit, sugar and a few other bits and pieces. The mixture is then wrapped in a dish cloth (clout), the ends tied together, and then boiled until ready. It's absolutely delicious, hot, cold, with cream or custard and in Glasgow and the West Coast it's even fried.

Edinburgh & the Borders

Prices
Approximate prices per room per night regardless of occupancy
£ = under £40
££ = £40–80
£££ = over £80

Room Rates
Hotels and guest-houses will have a board displaying room prices, usually double and single referring to the number of people sharing a room. Payment is per person so even if you are given a double room you will only be charged the single rate. If you're travelling in a group look out for family rooms which often work out cheaper per person.

Edinburgh

Amaryllis (£)
A friendly guest-house in a quiet residential street, yet close to the city centre.
✉ 21 Upper Gilmore Place
☎ 0131 229 3293; fax: 0131 229 3293

Apex International (£)
Situated in the heart of the Old Town with superb views of the Castle and close to lots of nightlife.
✉ 31–5 Grassmarket ☎ 0131 300 3456; fax: 0131 220 5345

Balmoral (£££)
Sir Rocco Forte's flagship hotel is an imposing Edwardian building overlooking the east end of Princes Street.
✉ 1 Princes Street ☎ 0131 556 2414; fax: 0131 557 3747

Bonham (££)
A Victorian town house on the edge of the quaint Dean Village and minutes from Princes Street. Each of the bedrooms features an individual design.
✉ 35 Drumsheugh Gardens
☎ 0131 226 6050; fax: 0131 226 6080

Caledonian (£££)
This fine example of Victorian high living is the most impressive building on Princes Street. Constructed of Dumfriesshire sandstone this is where you are most likely to meet Sean Connery when he is in town.
✉ Princes Street ☎ 0131 459 9988; fax: 0131 225 6632

Channings (££)
Scottish cooking is a speciality at Channings, a stylish transformation of five Edwardian town houses on a cobbled street overlooking gardens.
✉ South Learmonth Gardens
☎ 0131 315 2226; fax: 0131 332 9631

The George Inter-Continental (£££)
Georgian elegance complete with Corinthian pillars, a marble floored foyer and two of the best restaurants in Edinburgh, one serving superb French food.
✉ 19–21 George Street
☎ 0131 225 1251; fax: 0131 226 5644

Greens (£)
This conversion of four Georgian houses in the West End of the New Town is a most comfortable place to stay. The Bistro offers an informal food option to the Garden Restaurant.
✉ 24 Eglinton Crescent
☎ 0131 337 1565; fax: 0131 346 2990

Hilton National (£££)
Modern, friendly, good-value hotel in the busy West End. Handy for the Haymarket rail station and a few minutes' walk from Princes Street.
✉ 69 Belford Road ☎ 0131 332 2545; fax: 0131 332 3805

Ibis (£)
Situated in a trendy square just off the Royal Mile with practical modern rooms, self-service breakfast and close to several excellent restaurants.
✉ 6 Hunter Square ☎ 0131 240 7000; fax: 0131 240 7007

Sheraton Grand (£££)
An imposing modern luxury hotel complete with marble entrance hall, floodlit views of the castle from its Terrace

Restaurant and an excellent reputation for fine Scottish cuisine.

✉ 1 Festival Square ☎ 0131 229 9131; fax: 0131 228 4510

The Town House (£)
An elegant former manse just 10 minutes from Princes Street, combining comfortable accommodation with friendly service and an awesome breakfast.

✉ 65 Gilmore Place ☎ 0131 229 1985

The Borders

Biggar
Shieldhill Country House Hotel (££)
An 800-year-old castle in 2.5ha of parkland with a 12th-century oak-panelled lounge, four-posters in all bedrooms and award-winning Scottish cuisine.

✉ Quothquan ☎ 01899 220035; fax: 01899 221092

Gullane
Greywalls (£££)
Designed in 1901 by Sir Edwin Lutyens, Architect of New Delhi, it is the only remaining Lutyen's house in Scotland. The garden was created by Gertrude Jekyll, and next door is the championship golf course of Muirfield.

✉ Muirfield ☎ 01620 842144; fax: 01620 842241

Jedburgh
Spread Eagle House (£)
A small but comfortable hotel in the heart of one of Scotland's most historic towns.

✉ High Street ☎ 01835 862870

Kenmore Bank Hotel (£)
Family-run guest-house with grand views of the Jed Water and the towering bulk of Jedburgh Abbey.

✉ Oxnam Road ☎ 01835 862369; fax 01835 862112

Kelso
Cross Keys (££)
One of the prominent features on Kelso's cobbled square, this Georgian reconstruction of an old coaching inn is a superb base for touring.

✉ 36–7 The Square ☎ 01573 223303; fax: 01573 225792

Melrose
Burts (££)
This early 18th-century building is the place to experience the best of 'Scotland's Natural Larder', not to mention an interesting selection of malt whiskies.

✉ Market Square ☎ 01896 822285; fax: 01896 822870

George and Abbotsford Hotel (££)
An 18th-century former coaching inn with a good selection of bar meals, situated in an exceedingly pretty Borders town near Sir Walter Scott's Abbotsford.

✉ High Street ☎ 01896 822308; fax: 01896 823363

Peebles
Peebles Hotel Hydro (£££)
An absolute gem of a hotel with fine food, a beautiful view and lots of activities.

✉ On the A702 just outside town ☎ 01721 720602; fax: 01721 722999

Whitestone House (£)
A former manse which is friendly, warm, reasonably priced and with decent-sized comfortable rooms.

✉ Innerleithen Road ☎ 01721 720337

St Boswells
Dryburgh Abbey Hotel (££)
This Baronial mansion is situated on the banks of the Tweed across from Dryburgh Abbey, with its own swimming-pool and an extensive wine list.

✉ Off the B6356 ☎ 01835 822261; fax: 01835 823945

Bed and Breakfast
This type of accommodation can range from properties with all the facilities of a small hotel to the spare room in a crofter's house. You can find them in directories of accommodation or through the local Tourist Information Centre. But the fun way is to drive or walk around until you see a vacancy sign outside a house you like the look of and knock on the door.

Glasgow & the Southwest

Breakfast

The great Scottish breakfast is usually included in the price of overnight accommodation in less expensive establishments, but not always, so it's wise to check when booking. In middle- to top-range hotels, breakfast will be extra and can be expensive. A good idea is to skip breakfast when staying in such a place and seek out a small local café where, for a fraction of the cost, you will get far better value.

Glasgow

Botanic Hotel (£)

Attractive Victorian terrace house in the West End close to the Botanic Gardens, Kelvingrove and the transport museum.

✉ **1 Alfred Terrace** ☎ **0141 339 6955; fax: 0141 337 1812**

Devonshire Hotel (£££)

Victorian elegance in a secluded tree-lined terrace, yet minutes from many major attractions. First-class restaurant.

✉ **5 Devonshire Gardens** ☎ **0141 339 7878; fax: 0141 339 2001**

Ewington Hotel (££)

A south-side Best Western town house serving international cuisine. Close to the Burrell Collection, it's only six minutes by train to the city centre.

✉ **Balmoral Terrace, 132 Queens Drive** ☎ **0141 423 1152; fax: 0141 422 2030**

Glasgow Hilton (£££)

This is where it's at in Glasgow. Minski's Deli is modelled on the New York original and Raffles Bar looks like the one in Singapore. Great views and service.

✉ **1 William Street** ☎ **0141 204 5555; fax: 0141 204 5004**

Greek Thomson Hotel (££)

Near Charing Cross and Sauchiehall Street, serving a particularly good Scottish breakfast with portions large enough to ensure you won't need lunch.

✉ **140 Elderslie Street** ☎ **0141 332 6556**

Jury's (££)

Popular West End leisure hotel used to catering to visitors to the city. Ideal for the Botanic Gardens, Kelvingrove and the Museum of Transport.

✉ **Great Western Road** ☎ **0141 334 8161; fax: 0141 334 3846**

Millennium Hotel (££££)

Situated in the heart of the city close to all major attractions, excellent restaurants and the vibrant Glasgow nightlife.

✉ **40 George Square** ☎ **0141 332 6711; fax: 0141 332 4264**

One Devonshire Gardens (£££)

If you are looking for something elegant and sophisticated yet different, with legendary French and Scottish cuisine, stay here.

✉ **1 Devonshire Gardens** ☎ **0141 339 2001; fax: 0141 337 1663**

The Thistle (£££)

Superb hotel favoured by the Prime Minister, Tony Blair, just behind Sauchiehall Street, close to the School of Art, the Willow Tea Room and the Royal Concert Hall.

✉ **36 Cambridge Street** ☎ **0870 333 9154; fax 0870 333 9254**

The Southwest

Auchencairn

Balcary Bay (££)

A 17th-century country house hotel on a picturesque bay. Scottish cuisine is based on local produce.

✉ **Near Castle Douglas** ☎ **01556 640217; fax: 01556 640272**

Ayr

Fairfield House (££)

There are fine views over the

Firth of Clyde to Arran from this Victorian mansion which is close to the town centre and within easy travelling of the Robert Burns National Heritage Park.

✉ 12 Fairfield Road ☎ 01292 267461; fax: 01292 261456

Beattock
Auchen Castle (££)
A 19th-century mansion in a garden and woodland setting. Private trout loch and award-winning restaurant.

✉ South of Moffat off the A74 ☎ 01683 300407; fax: 01683 300667

Castle Douglas
Douglas Arms (£)
Situated in the centre of this market town this former coaching inn is a great favourite with local people for the friendliness of its staff.

✉ King Street ☎ 01556 502231; fax: 01556 504000

Urr Valley Country House (£)
Country-house hotel on the outskirts of town. The wood-panelled lounge has fishing trophies and roaring log fires.

✉ Ernespie Road ☎ 01556 502188; fax: 01556 504055

Kirkcudbright
Royal (£)
Comfortable, reasonably priced hotel in the centre of this artists' colony. Very good base for exploring the Solway coast.

✉ St Cuthbert Street ☎ 01557 331213; fax: 01557 331513

Selkirk Arms (££)
Lord Peter Wimsey, Dorothy L Sayer's fictional detective, lodged in this fine 18th-century hotel in the novel *The Five Red Herrings*. Robert Burns wrote his famous *Selkirk Grace* while staying here.

✉ Old High Street ☎ 01557 330402; fax: 01557 331639

Moffat
The Star (£)
This wonderful little hotel appears in the *Guinness Book of Records* as the narrowest hotel in the world.

✉ 44 High Street ☎ 01683 220156; fax: 01683 221524

Newton Stewart
Kirroughtree House (££)
A 17th-century mansion in a Galloway countryside setting, the Kirroughtree is a superb time capsule of a more gracious and elegant age.

✉ Minnigaff ☎ 01671 402141; fax: 01671 402425

Portpatrick
Fernhill (££)
Dramatically perched on a hill overlooking the picturesque harbour and village of Portpatrick, Fernhill is situated at the start of the Southern Upland Way.

✉ Heugh Road ☎ 01776 810220; fax: 01776 810596

Stranraer
North West Castle (££)
The former home of 19th-century Arctic explorer Sir John Ross has its own swimming-pool and ice-rink.

✉ On the Seafront ☎ 01776 704413; fax: 01776 702646

Thornhill
Trigony House (££)
Former Edwardian hunting lodge set in secluded gardens and famed locally for its ambience and cuisine.

✉ Closeburn (1.5km/1 mile south off the A76) ☎ 01848 331211; fax: 01848 331303

Turnberry
Westin Turnberry Hotel, Golf Courses and Spa (£££)
This world-famous hotel has the grandest outlook in Scotland. Its Ailsa golf course is probably the finest in the world.

✉ On the A719 ☎ 01655 331000; fax: 01655 331706

Credit Cards
Most of the well-known credit and debit cards are generally accepted by Scottish hotels and guest houses. Bed and breakfasts are a different story and although practice is changing there are still proprietors who want and expect to be paid in cash. Some will happily take traveller's cheques, but it is wise to ascertain the method of payment in advance. The same applies in restaurants.

Central Scotland

Hostels

A cheaper alternative accommodation for people on a tight budget is the network of Youth and Backpackers Hostels. They provide simple lodgings (usually in dormitories), cooking and washing facilities and the opportunity to meet fellow travellers. The Scottish Youth Hostel Association (☎ 01786 891400) has an extensive network of properties ranging from old schools and croft houses to a splendid Highland castle.

Arduaine

Loch Melfort Hotel (££)
Glorious views over Loch Melfort and down the Sound of Jura, combined with award-winning cuisine featuring the best of fresh local produce.
✉ On the A816 midway between Oban and Lochgilphead ☎ 01852 200233; fax: 01852 200214

Auchterarder

The Gleneagles Hotel (£££)
Beautiful countryside, outstanding range of activities and first-class cuisine make this one of the world's top hotels.
✉ On the A823 ☎ 01764 662231; fax: 01764 662134

Crail

Balcomie Links (£)
Friendly, good-value, family-run hotel near the golf course in Fife's most picturesque coastal village.
✉ Balcomie Road ☎ 01333 450237; fax: 01333 450540

Crief

Crieff Hydro (££)
Set in 365ha of Perthshire countryside with a unique combination of leisure facilities and accommodation.
✉ Ferntower Road ☎ 01764 655555; fax: 01764 653087

Dundee

Hilton (£££)
Next to Discovery Point, with bedrooms overlooking the Tay: the best place in town.
✉ Earl Grey Place ☎ 01382 229271; fax: 01382 200072

Swallow (££)
On the outskirts of Dundee, this comfortable hotel is within easy travelling of Perth and central Scotland.
✉ Kingsway West, Invergowrie ☎ 01382 631200; fax: 01382 631201

Killiecrankie

Killiecrankie (££)
Nineteenth-century country manse overlooking the River Garry and the historic Pass of Killiecrankie. Close to Blair Castle, Pitlochry and Perth.
✉ West of Killiecrankie on the B8019 ☎ 01796 473220; fax: 01796 472451

Perth

Kinfauns Castle (£££)
Distinctive Scottish cuisine prepared by an award-winning team is the hallmark of this superb hotel.
✉ Kinfauns ☎ 01738 620777; fax: 01738 620778

St Andrews

The Old Course Hotel (££££)
Situated as close to the 17th hole of the world's most famous golf course as you can get without playing it.
✉ 40 The Scores ☎ 01334 474371; fax: 01334 477668

Taynuilt

Taychreggan Hotel (££)
A remote place of tranquillity and natural beauty overlooking Loch Awe. Famous for its collection of malt whiskies.
✉ From the A85 take the B845 at Taynuilt to Kilchrenan and Taychreggan ☎ 01866 833211; fax: 01866 833244

Tobermory, Isle of Mull

Western Isles Hotel (££)
Overlooking Tobermory Bay with its coloured houses and one of the best views in the Hebrides.
✉ Above the town ☎ 01688 302012; fax: 01688 302297

The North

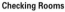

Aberdeen
Travel Inn (£)
Cheap and cheerful modern accommodation. If you're on a budget this is a good base for touring the North.

✉ **Murcar, Bridge of Don** ☎ **01224 821217; fax: 01224 706869**

Ballater
Balgonie House Hotel (££)
Set in 1.5ha of mature gardens, overlooking Ballater golf course in the heart of Royal Deeside, this friendly hotel has an excellent reputation for specialised Scottish cuisine.

✉ **Braemar Place** ☎ **013397 55482; fax: 01339 755482**

Inverness
Dunain Park (£££)
Georgian country house with award-winning restaurant in 2.5ha of garden and woodlands, close to the town.

✉ **On the A82** ☎ **01463 230512; fax: 01463 224532**

Kirkwall, Orkney
Ayre Hotel (££)
Relaxed seafront hotel offering the best of local ingredients in its superb restaurant. Also home to the now-legendary Saturday night Ayre Hotel folk sessions, featuring some of Orkney's most talented musicians.

✉ **Ayre Road** ☎ **01856 873001; fax: 01856 876289**

Lerwick, Shetland
Glen Orchy House (££)
A luxury conversion from an old convent building. The home-cooked dinners are excellent and the breakfasts awesome. This is the best place to stay on the islands.

✉ **20 Knab Road** ☎ **01595 692031; fax: 01595 692031**

Muir of Ord
The Dower House (££)
Early 18th-century building in secluded gardens. Well placed for Royal Dornoch, Nairn and other golf courses, and as a touring centre for Loch Ness, Glen Affric, Cromarty and the West.

✉ **Highfield** ☎ **01463 870090; fax: 01463 870090**

Onich
The Lodge on The Loch Hotel (££)
This is one of the most spectacular lochside settings in the Highlands, offering a connoisseur selection of malt whiskies, wild salmon, venison and game and particularly legendary home-baking.

✉ **On A82, 16km (10 miles) south of Fort William** ☎ **01855 821237; fax: 01855 821463**

Stornoway, Isle of Lewis
Cabarfeidh (££)
Friendly, popular hotel with French cuisine. From here you can explore the Western Isles.

✉ **On the edge of town** ☎ **01851 702604; fax: 01851 705572**

Ullapool
The Ceilidh Place (£–££)
Warm, friendly, cosy and probably the best place to stay while exploring the Western Highlands. As well as superb Scottish food in the coffee shop or the more formal restaurant, the Ceilidh Place has it's own bookshop and budget accommodation in the adjacent clubhouse. This is *the* place to hear folk music in the Highlands.

✉ **West Argyll Street** ☎ **01854 612103; fax: 01854 612886**

Checking Rooms
When inquiring about accommodation in a hotel or bed and breakfast, it is perfectly acceptable to ask to see the room before committing yourself. There are some establishments which look grand on the surface, but when you check in you discover you have the room from Hell. Avoid this by having a quick inspection and if you don't like what you see just say it's not what you're looking for.

Shopping in Scotland

The Rag Trade

The Scottish Borders are the centre of the country's textile industry, producing a range of fabrics including wool, cashmere and tweed. Clothing manufactured in the Borders is available throughout Scotland, but because many of the mills and factories have shops where they sell seconds and factory rejects, the best bargains can often be found here. Most shops also sell perfect quality goods at discounted prices.

Tweeds, Tartans, Lace and Woollies

Edinburgh

MacPhersons of Edinburgh
Kiltmakers and Highland outfitters of distinction.
✉ **17 West Maitland Street, Haymarket** ☎ **0131 225 4008; fax 0131 225 9823**

Geoffrey (Tailor)
This is the best source of tartan in all of Edinburgh. Kilts, both for men and women, off-the-peg or made-to-measure, plus a fair selection of ex-hire garments for sale and all the usual accessories at a reasonable price.
✉ **57–9 High Street** ☎ **0131 557 0256; fax 0131 556 0615**

John Morrison
Good selection of tweeds and tartans, including ready-to-wear ladies' and gents' kilts.
✉ **462 Lawnmarket, Royal Mile** ☎ **0131 225 8149**

Hawick

Chas N Whillans
Own-label cashmere and lambswool sweaters. Also sells goods manufactured by Pringle, Lyle & Scott and Barrie, and a range of leisure- and golfwear, including Nick Faldo, Alice Collins and Barbour.
✉ **Teviotdale Mills, Albert Road** ☎ **01450 373128**

Peter Scott
Established over a century ago, this local firm specialises in knitwear for men and women, from top-quality wool and cashmere.
✉ **11 Buccleuch Street** ☎ **01450 372311; fax 01450 374610**

Wrights of Trowmill
Wide range of coats, caps, travel rugs and skirts in wool and tweed.
✉ **Trowmill** ☎ **01450 372555; fax 01450 377663**

Kilmarnock

Jaeger
Famous-name factory shop in the home town of Johnnie Walker whisky. Sells the full range, from men's suits to ladies' blouses.
✉ **15 Munro Place, Bonnyton Industrial Estate** ☎ **01563 526511; fax 01563 540846**

Newmilns (Ayrshire)

Moonweave Mill Shop
Situated in the Irvine Valley, last bastion of UK lace production, this factory shops sells curtains, table covers, bedspreads and blankets.
✉ **Stoneygate Road** ☎ **01560 321216; fax 01560 323071**

Crafts and Gift Shops

Crieff

Crieff Visitors Centre
Offers a wide selection of ceramics, including mugs, plates and tea and coffee pots.
✉ **Muthill Road** ☎ **01764 654014**

Stuart Crystal
Factory shop selling both seconds and perfects. Lead crystal glasses, decanters and giftware. Also some Waterford crystal and Wedgwood.
✉ **Muthill Road** ☎ **01764 654004**

Dunoon

Dunoon Ceramics
Dunoon mugs, available in

gift shops throughout Scotland, make great gifts to take home. Buy them here for great discounts on end-of-line bargains and seconds.

✉ **Hamilton Street** ☎ **01369 704360**

Moniaive
The Green Tea House
This organic café incorporates a selection of arts and crafts by local artists. Sanquhar knitting kits, aromatherapy oils, ethnic clothes, candles, honey and pottery.

✉ **Chapel Street** ☎ **01848 200131**

Oban
Caithness Glass
One of many outlets for Caithness glass, with a good selection of crystal glasses, tableware and some great ideas for gifts.

✉ **Waterfront Centre, Railway Pier**
☎ **01631 563386**

Pitlochry
Heathergems
If you've bought the tartan, here's where you get the heather. Jewellery made from dried heather, set in silver and pewter and featuring Celtic designs.

✉ **22 Atholl Road** ☎ **01796 473863**

St Andrews
Heritage Golf
Golf clubs, carts and accessories, plus sweaters and waterproofs. Also some 19th-century reproduction clubs. Just the job for a new niblick.

✉ **Argyll Business Park, Largo Road**
☎ **01334 472266**

Selkirk
Selkirk Glass
Glass paperweights, ornaments, animals and hand-painted pottery.

✉ **Dunsdale Haugh** ☎ **01750 20954**

Thornhill (Dumfries & Galloway)
Drumlanrig
This craft centre has a series of small shops specialising in crafts, including leather and jewellery.

✉ **Drumlanrig Castle**
☎ **01848 330248**

Ullapool
Highland Stoneware
Hand-painted pottery and stoneware with an enormous selection of table- and cookware, as well as the more decorative gift items.

✉ **Mill Street** ☎ **01854 612980**

Antiques and Collectables

Edinburgh
Byzantium
Antique-cum-flea market. An eclectic collection of shops in one building, with a café/restaurant on the top floor.

✉ **9 Victoria Street** ☎ **0131 225 1768**

Carson Clark
A seriously dangerous shop for those addicted to antique prints and maps. Wonderful, hand-painted reproductions, particularly of Old Edinburgh.

✉ **181–3 Canongate** ☎ **0131 556 4710**

Dead Head Comics
Early *Superman* comics, adventure, science fiction.

✉ **27 Candlemaker Row**
☎ **0131 226 2774**

The Grassmarket
The Grassmarket is probably the most concentrated area for antiques, collectables, second-hand clothes and books in Edinburgh. Here you will find that rare Scottish book, hand-tailored Norfolk shooting jacket or elegant cocktail dress. Or perhaps you would rather have an ancient claymore, some 1960s ephemera or back copies of long forgotten comics.

Singer Songwriter
Adam McNaughton is one of Scotland's best-known songwriters. His 'Jeely Piece Song' which laments the demise of the Glasgow tradition of throwing jam sandwiches from the upper floors of tenement buildings is his most popular work, followed by a humorous adaptation, in Glaswegian, of Shakespeare's *Hamlet*. But he also has a serious side, which is evident from his latest CD.

Greyfriars Antiques
One of many city antique shops, with a wide and varied selection.
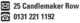 **25 Candlemaker Row**
☎ **0131 221 1192**

Glasgow
All Our Yesterdays
Interesting bric-à-brac and collectables from the not-too-distant past.
✉ **6 Park Road** ☎ **0141 334 7788**

Forbidden Planet
The Glasgow mecca for comic collectors.
✉ **168 Buchanan Street**
☎ **0141 331 1215**

Victorian Village
Another indoor shopping mall for antique lovers. You'll find everything here from 1950s comic annuals through fine antique prints and paintings to exquisite jewellery.
✉ **57 West Regent Street**
☎ **0141 332 9808**

Books

Edinburgh
Bauermeister
Stretching along the street from the Central Library, this series of book and record shops is the one to head for. Make for the end nearest the National Museum where you will find their comprehensive selection of Scottish and local books.
✉ **19 George IV Bridge**
☎ **0131 226 5561**

Broughton Books
One of the best book shops in Edinburgh. You can spend hours browsing here.
✉ **2a Broughton Place**
☎ **0131 557 8010**

McNaughtan's Bookshop
Another dark and inviting place where a casual browse can often unearth a real gem or a bargain.
✉ **3a Haddington Place, Leith Walk**
☎ **0131 556 5897**

Glasgow
Border Books
Get lost for hours, even days, in this enormous literary emporium. Every book you ever wanted is here, or can be ordered.
✉ **98 Buchanan Street**
☎ **0141 222 7700**

Voltaire & Rousseau
This is the longest running secondhand bookshop in Glasgow and an absolute must see for anyone interested in books.
✉ **Otago Lane** ☎ **0141 339 1811**

Whisky

Edinburgh
Royal Mile Whiskies
If you can resist the mouth-watering window display you don't need to buy whisky. Opposite St Giles Cathedral.
✉ **379 High Street** ☎ **0131 225 3383**

William Cadenhead
Tucked away at the bottom of the Royal Mile, this small shop has a great selection of whiskies. You can even buy a whole barrel of the stuff.
✉ **172 Canongate** ☎ **0131 556 5864**

Dufftown
The Whisky Shop
Stock up here from a wide selection of local whiskies, although if you have the time

you could tour all the distilleries instead.

✉ **1 Fife Street** ☎ **01340 821097**

Wigtown
Bladnoch Distillery

Most southerly distillery in Scotland, closed for a number of years but now producing a limited amount. In the meantime enjoy the tour and rejoice in the knowledge that the owner has captured all remaining stocks of this unique malt and has them for sale in the shop.

✉ **Bladnoch, Wigtown** ☎ **01988 402605**

Orkney
Highland Park Distillery

The Orcadian version of 'The Water of Life'.

✉ **Kirkwall** ☎ **01856 874619**

Food

Edinburgh
Charles MacSween & Son

MacSween haggis is available in shops and supermarkets all over Scotland, but this is the source. Try their vegetarian version with nuts and pulses.

✉ **118 Bruntsfield Place** ☎ **0131 229 1216**

Ian Mellis

A traditional cheesemonger whose shop you will smell before you see. Stocks the most amazing range of Scottish cheeses including Loch Arthur, Dunsyre Blue, Dunlop and Tobermory cheddar. You can smell and sample the stuff before you decide what to buy. Do not miss the best oat-cakes in the world, also available here.

✉ **30 Victoria Street** ☎ **0131 226 6215**

Valvona and Crolla

Scotland has a sizeable Italian community and this is where they come to shop. Fresh produce is shipped in weekly from Italy. Here you can get everything from haggis to fettucini. The café is one of the hidden delights of the capital.

✉ **19 Elm Row** ☎ **0131 556 6066**

Glasgow
Peckhams

Amazing deli stocking a wide range of Scottish produce, and open until late. Just the job for a spot of last-minute shopping before you leave. The Edinburgh branch is at Waverley station.

✉ **61–65 Glassford Street** ☎ **0141 553 0666**

Aberlour on Spey
Walkers Shortbread

Famous tartan shortbread, in packets and tins with a picture of Bonnie Prince Charlie on the front, is made here and you can buy it fresh from the factory shop as well as a complete range of oatcakes, cakes and biscuits.

✉ **Aberlour** ☎ **01340 871555**

Fochabers
Baxters

This is *the* place to buy Mrs Baxter's celebrated products. There's a full range of soups, jams and preserves, along with great gift ideas in the Cookshop. Try the factory tour before deciding what to buy, then follow up with lunch in the self-service restaurant.

✉ **Baxters Visitor Centre** ☎ **01343 820666**

Whisky

Investigate the mysteries and traditions of Scotch whisky without going near a single distillery. The Whisky Heritage Centre at the top of Edinburgh's Royal Mile is just the place to learn all about Scotland's national drink. Ride through 300 years of history in a barrel cart, passing life-like figures and taking in the authentic sounds and smells of the distilling process. Then head for the bar and have a wee taste yourself or buy a bottle from the well stocked shop.

Children's Attractions

Fun for Children

Scotland is a fascinating place for children. While there are attractions specifically geared to them, many other places will have undoubted apeal. The imaginative child will have a great time exploring old battlefields and ruined castles, while the more studious will be difficult to dislodge from the hundreds of museums. But whatever their tastes, all children will enjoy the leisure centres, swimming-pools, beaches and country parks which can be found throughout Scotland.

Edinburgh

Brass Rubbing Centre

A 15th-century college church with Pictish crosses. Instructions and equipment provided.

✉ **Trinity Apse, Chalmers Close, Royal Mile (opposite Museum of Childhood)**
☎ **0131 556 4364**

Butterfly and Insect World

Exotic rainforest setting for butterflies from around the world, plus some interesting creepy crawlies and a nearby Bird of Prey Centre.

✉ **Dobbies Garden World, Lasswade** ☎ **0131 663 4932**

Dynamic Earth

This geological visitors' centre tells the story of our planet using special effects and the lastest in interactive technology. Witness meteor showers, see volcanoes erupting and visit tropical rainforests. There are computer programes and information boards for younger children.

✉ **William Younger Centre, Holyrood** ☎ **0131 550 7800**

Edinburgh Zoo

One of the top zoos in Britain, set in hillside parkland. It has the world's largest penguin enclosure with a 'Penguin Parade' daily at 2PM.

✉ **Corstorphine Road**
☎ **0131 334 9171**

Gorgie City Farm

Goats, ducks, pigs and hens, along with a cow and a Shetland pony in a community farm 10 minutes from Princes Street.

✉ **51 Gorgie Road** ☎ **0131 337 4202**

Museum of Childhood

Superb free facility with toys from yesteryear. Show your children that there was life before playstations were invented.

✉ **42 High Street, Royal Mile**
☎ **0131 529 4142**

Glasgow

Glasgow Zoo

The developing, open-plan zoo has birds, mammals and reptiles housed in spacious enclosures and buildings.

✉ **Uddingston (east of Glasgow, signposted off the M74)** ☎ **0141 771 1185**

Aberdeen

Codona's Amusement Park

Scotland's largest amusement park, with lots of major rides, kiddie rides, adventure playground, video games and a roller-coaster. Admission fee buys a wristband giving unlimited access. Very good value for money.

✉ **Beach Boulevard**
☎ **01224 595910**

Beach Leisure Complex

With one of the longest enclosed flumes in the world, this is a must for the family. There is also an exotic leisure pool, three more flumes and a massive ice-rink which offers skating and ice discos.

✉ **Beach Promenade**
☎ **01224 655401**

Jonah's Journey

Take a trip into the belly of a whale. This fascinating activity-based learning centre is ideal for children and they can discover all sorts of information about life in biblical times. They get to dress up, grind grain, spin and weave, visit the local well and go into a nomad's tent and an Israelite house.

120 Rosemount Place
☎ 01224 647614

Aviemore
Highland Wildlife Park
Drive-through reserve featuring Scottish mammals and birds of the past and present including red deer, bison and Highland cattle. A walk-round area has capercaillie, eagles, wolves and wildcats.

✉ Off the A9 (B9152), 4.5km (7 miles) south of Aviemore
☎ 01540 651270

Biggar
Puppet Theatre
A miniature Victorian theatre with seating for a hundred. Performances, including a very entertaining version of the Loch Ness Monster, displays and guided tours backstage.

✉ On the B7016 east of town
☎ 01899 220631

Dundee
Shaws Sweet Factory
Old-fashioned sweets are made in this 1940s factory using traditional techniques such as striping and sugar pulling. Demonstrations and explanations from the sweetmaker and a taster, of course.

✉ Old Keiller Buildings, 34 Mains Loan
☎ 01382 461435

Girvan
Ailsa Craig
This granite island is 13km (8 miles) off the Ayrshire coast and accessible by boat from Girvan. The source of all the world's curling stones and a bird sanctuary, it is hugely popular with children, not to mention adults.

✉ Mark McCrindle at Girvan Harbour
☎ 01465 713219

Linlithgow
Beecraigs Country Park
Woodland walks, a deer farm, a fish farm and a host of activities including archery.

✉ Take the Preston road and follow signs
☎ 01506 844516

Melrose
Teddy Melrose
A teddy bear museum featuring some exceedingly famous bears such as Rupert, Paddington and Pooh.

✉ The Wynd
☎ 01896 823854

Skye
Serpentarium
There are more reptiles under one roof than you could ever imagine. Snakes, tortoises, frogs and lizards. Kids go crazy over them.

✉ The Old Mill, Harrapool, Broadford
☎ 01471 822209

Stirling
Blair Drummond Safari Leisure Park
You can drive through this wild animal reserve, with Chimp Island, performing sea lions and walk-round pet farm.

✉ Exit 10 of the M9, north of Stirling
☎ 01786 841456

Strathpeffer
Highland Museum of Childhood
This is what life was like for children in the Highlands in past times, brought to life by the displays. Quizzes for kids, plus a regular programme of events and activities.

✉ The Old Station
☎ 01997 421031

Scottish Folk Festivals
From Easter to November you will find a folk festival of some sort taking place nearly every weekend. Usually held in small towns and villages, they have an intimate, party atmosphere and children love them, not just because there is usually some entertainment aimed at them, but because there are lots of other children and new friends are easily made.

Discos, Pubs and Nightclubs

The Glasgow Scene

While you will find nightclubs throughout Scotland, the very best can be found in Glasgow, which has more culture per square metre than most cities in Europe. The nightclub scene proper starts very late, and before that everyone hangs out in the pubs. If you're on a tight budget head for the clubs before 10PM and you might get a discount or free entry. Smart dress is essential, and definitely no sneakers or trainers.

Edinburgh

Fingers Piano Bar
A late, late club with blues, pop and rock, nightly till 3AM.
✉ **Frederick Street, below Chez Jules Restaurant** ☎ **0131 225 3026**

Honeycomb
Mixture of house and garage music, plus live jazz.
✉ **15–17 Niddry Street**
☎ **0131 530 5540**

La Belle Angèle
The music changes every night, but check for details of when to find soul, hip hop, Latin, jazz or house.
✉ **11 Hasties Close** ☎ **0131 225 7536**

Negociants
Live bands in the basement until 1AM in this French-style café-bar which serves great coffee and croissants upstairs.
✉ **45 Lothian Street** ☎ **0131 225 6313**

Nobles Bar
Victorian pub setting near the newly gentrified dock area. Magnificent horseshoe bar featuring regular live jazz sessions.
✉ **44a Constitution Street, Leith** ☎ **0131 553 3873**

The Venue
Popular night-spot behind Waverley Station where you can find, on different nights, everything from house, garage and funk to '70s disco.
✉ **15 Calton Road** ☎ **0131 554 2024**

Glasgow

The Cathouse
If hard rock is your bag this is *the* club for you.
✉ **15 Union Street** ☎ **0141 248 6606**

Curlers
Favourite of students from the nearby University, and also a few BBC types. Live music includes jazz and folk midweek, with student bands performing at the weekend.
✉ **Byers Road** ☎ **0141 338 6511**

The Garage
You'll recognise this one by the vehicle protruding from the wall above the door. University halls of residence are situated close by so this has become a popular student haunt playing disco music from the '70s, '80s and '90s.
✉ **490 Sauchiehall Street**
☎ **0141 332 1120**

King Tut's Wah Wah Hut
Live music most nights featuring local and national bands and the occasional very big name.
✉ **272 St Vincent Street**
☎ **0141 221 5279**

The Riverside Club
This is a famous Glasgow dance venue, but don't expect disco. This is where the great craze in Scottish ceilidh dancing started, and not the refined version of the Scottish Country Dance Association either. This is a living tradition and it doesn't matter if you don't know the steps or the dances, you'll soon pick them up or make them up. Wonderful fun and great to see hordes of young people queuing to get in.
✉ **Just off Clyde Street**
☎ **0141 248 3144**

Victoria's
Two discos, a piano bar with a resident cabaret and regular appearances by some of Scotland's top artistes. This sophisticated venue attracts smart people from a wide range of ages. British Nightclub of the Year 1996.

✉ **98 Sauchiehall Street**
☎ **0141 332 1444**

Celtic Music
This music is the traditional music from the seven Celtic countries – Scotland, Ireland, Wales, Isle of Man, Cornwall, Brittany and Galicia. Each country has its own unique sound, but overall there is a thread running through the music that identifies it as Celtic. As a living tradition it is constantly changing, and travelling musicians from the various areas, as well as from non-Celtic countries are taking the music, adapting and adding to it, then passing it back. So it's not surprising to hear Galician or Breton tunes played by Scottish musicians in an Edinburgh pub, nor to hear the strains of an Irish lament played in the square of the great cathedral of Santiago de Compostela. When you head to your first session don't try to analyse or even understand it. Just enjoy it.

Edinburgh
Sandy Bells Bar
It's actually called the Forrest Hill Bar, but a previous manager was called Sandy Bell and the name stuck. Even the brewers now call it that. Once it was the best place in the entire universe to hear folk music, often played by international names joining in with the locals; now it's a bit quieter but still a great pub with some incredible sessions.

✉ **Forrest Road** ☎ **0131 225 2751**

The Tass
Another fine Edinburgh folk pub, featuring sessions on Thursday and Saturday nights and Sunday afternoons. Great grub and real ales the rest of the time.

✉ **Corner of High Street and St Mary's Street** ☎ **0131 556 6338**

The Royal Oak
Amazing ancient pub with regular sessions. The bar is one of the finest in Edinburgh, compact and cosy with a real fire. This is what pubs used to be like 40 years ago. Check the board outside for what's coming up and when.

✉ **Infirmary Street** ☎ **0131 557 2976**

Glasgow
The Scotia Bar
The favoured hang-out of writers and folkies. Billy Connolly used to drink here, and James Kelman (Booker prizewinner) is a regular. There are folk sessions on Wednesday nights and Saturday afternoons, but its also good for blues, poetry and a great atmosphere.

✉ **112 Stockwell Street**
☎ **0141 552 8681**

Victoria Bar
Just round the corner from the Scotia this is another favourite haunt of Glasgow musicians. The weekend is the best time for sessions.

✉ **57 Bridgegate** ☎ **0141 552 6040**

Celtic Music Pubs and Clubs
The bars and clubs where informal music sessions take place are by far the best places to hear genuine traditional Celtic music. Musicians and singers combine to produce an atmosphere that will make the hairs stand out on the back of your neck. But the spontaneity that makes a session so special also makes it a difficult beast to capture. Venues and dates change so check first before you venture forth.

Theatres

Dr Mavor and Mr Bridie

Osborn Henry Mavor, who trained and practised as a doctor, wrote plays under the pseudonym of James Bridie. He was instrumental in the founding of Glasgow's Citizen's Theatre and in 1950, the year before he died, founded Scotland's first College of Drama. His legacy includes a host of small touring companies and a thriving contemporary theatre scene.

Edinburgh
The Festival Theatre

Formerly the Empire and now refurbished, it is one of the city's top theatres with a greatly varied programme.

✉ **13–29 Nicholson Street**
☎ **0131 529 6000**

The King's

Magnificently refurbished, with a constantly changing popular programme and great pantos.

✉ **2 Leven Street, Tollcross**
☎ **0131 529 6000**

The Traverse

Small theatre with an international reputation for encouraging new drama.

✉ **10 Cambridge Street**
☎ **0131 228 1404**

Glasgow
The Citizens

One of the most influential theatres in Europe, with a magnificent, recently renovated auditorium. If you only have time to visit one theatre while in Scotland, make it this one.

✉ **119 Gorbals Street**
☎ **0141 429 0022**

Royal Concert Hall

Locals call it Lally's Palais, after the former Lord Provost Pat Lally. Hugely successful, with one of the most widely ranging programmes of concerts in Britain. Covering the entire spectrum from classical to jazz, it is also the venue, each January, for the innovative Celtic Connections Festival.

✉ **2 Sauchiehall Street**
☎ **0141 353 8000**

The Tron

Trendy and contemporary. Puts on some great music.

✉ **63 Trongate** ☎ **0141 552 4267**

Dumfries
Theatre Royal

Scotland's oldest working theatre. Robert Burns was a regular, as was J M Barrie. Dumfries native John Laurie (Private Fraser in *Dad's Army*) started his acting career here. It is run by the Guild of Players, a polished amateur dramatic society. There are occassional visits from touring companies.

✉ **66–8 Shakespeare Street**
☎ **01387 254209**

Dundee
Dundee Repertory Theatre

Lots of locally produced contemporary theatre seasoned by contributions from touring companies.

✉ **Tay Square** ☎ **01382 223530**

Inverness
Eden Court Theatre

This is the main venue in the Highlands covering everything from drama to music and dance.

✉ **Bishops Road** ☎ **01463 234234**

Mull
Mull Little Theatre

The smallest theatre in Scotland has only 43 seats but that doesn't affect the quality of the performances, and the atmosphere is terrific.

✉ **Dervaig** ☎ **01688 302828**

Pitlochry
Pitlochry Festival Theatre

Smashing 500-seater theatre with a great mix of modern and classical plays.

✉ **Port-Na-Craig** ☎ **01796 484626**

Sport

Edinburgh
Midlothian Ski Centre
This municipal facility, with its massive artificial, year-round slope, has equipment hire and inexpensive tuition. Advance booking is advised.
✉ **Hillend, on the A702 Edinburgh–Biggar Road**
☎ **0131 445 4433**

Leith Waterworld
More a water leisure centre than a pool, this is a great place to amuse kids on those wet days.
✉ **337 Easter Road, Leith**
☎ **0131 555 6000**

Meadowbank Stadium
The place for serious sports people. Athletics stadium, weights room, climbing wall, velodrome, football pitches and squash and badminton courts.
✉ **139 London Road** ☎ **0131 661 5351**

Pentland Hills Trekking Centre
Thirty minutes' drive from Princes Street will bring you to this country centre where Icelandic ponies transport you to the Pentland Hills.
✉ **Windy Gowl Farm, Carlops**
☎ **01968 661095**

Royal Commonwealth Pool
On the edge of Holyrood Park, this Olympic-standard pool is the biggest and most accessible in the city.
✉ **21 Dalkeith Road** ☎ **0131 667 7211**

Glasgow
Allander Sports Complex
Great family sports centre with pool, badminton, snooker and squash.
✉ **Milngavie Road, Bearsden**
☎ **0141 942 2233**

Dale's Bicycle Hire
Reasonable rates from one of the few hire shops in the city.
✉ **150 Dobbies Loan** ☎ **0141 332 2705**

Scotstoun Leisure Centre
Multi-sports complex, including swimming-pool and football pitches.
✉ **Danes Drive** ☎ **0141 959 4000**

Time Capsule
A short drive from Glasgow city centre, this combined pool and ice-rink, with various other leisure facilities thrown in, is a great hit with families.
✉ **100 Buchanan Street, Coatbridge** ☎ **01236 449572**

Dumfries
Ice Bowl
Offers ice-skating, curling and indoor bowls. A municipal facility with low prices.
✉ **King Street** ☎ **01387 251300**

Inverness
Aquadome
Flumes and a wave machine make this leisure pool a must for kids on a rainy day. For serious swimmers there's a competition pool and the usual health facilities, including massage and hydrotherapy.
✉ **Bught Park** ☎ **01463 667500**

Irvine
Magnum Leisure Centre
Huge centre with leisure pool, indoor ice-rink, squash, badminton, bowls and even a cinema.
✉ **Irvine Harbour** ☎ **01294 278381**

Cycle Trails in Glasgow
Glasgow is a great place to cycle, with miles of specially created tracks. Using old railway tracks and canal and riverside paths it's now possible to cycle from Glasgow to Edinburgh or Loch Lomond and even down the Clyde Coast. One of the best runs, though, is along the banks of the River Kelvin, starting from the Botanical Gardens.

What's On When

January
The Ba' Orkney. Very dangerous game of street football between two teams, the Uppies and the Downies, played through the streets of Kirkwall, seemingly with few rules.
Celtic Connections Royal Concert Hall, Glasgow. Three weeks of music and culture.
Up Helly Aa Lerwick, Shetland. Annual Viking Fire Festival which takes place on the last Tuesday in January irrespective of weather.
Robert Burns Night On the anniversary of the poet's birthday (25 January) people gather for a traditional Burns Supper of haggis, neeps and tatties, a few drams of whisky, poetry and song.

February
Scottish Curling Championship. Grown men, and women, hurl lumps of rock along ice.

March
Whuppity Stoorie Lanark. Winter is symbolically banished by children running round the church beating each other with paper weapons.

April
The Scottish Grand National Ayr Racecourse.
Edinburgh International Folk Festival.

May
Girvan Traditional Folk Festival. A picturesque fishing harbour, intimate concert venues with top performers and unbelievable pub sessions combine to make this *the* best small folk festival in Scotland. Mayday Bank Holiday weekend.

1 May
Beltane Fire Festival. Pagan goings on at Edinburgh's Calton Hill. Great fun.

June
Riding the Marches Various Border towns. Traditionally to check the boundaries of the common land.

July
World Flounder Tramping Championships Palnackie, Dumfriesshire. When the little fish tickle your feet you realise this is not as easy as it sounds (➤ 59).
Moniaive Gala. Picturesque Dumfriesshire village at its best. Procession followed by a fair, and in the evening a ceilidh dance.

August
Edinburgh Arts Festival, Fringe and Military Tattoo.

September
Braemar Highland Games. Many games during summer, but this is the one to see.

October
The National Mod. Gaeldom's competition showcase. A different Highland town is chosen as the venue each year.

30 November
St Andrew's Day.

31 December
Hogmanay. Seeing the old year out and the new one in. Traditional first-footing, visiting neighbours and friends with a bottle and something to eat, is dying out. Instead, parties are the trend with Edinburgh's Princes Street Gardens the venue for the world's largest.

Practical Matters

Before You Go	118
When You Are There	119–23
Language	124

UNI ÆQUUS VIRTUTI

Above: an Edinburgh
mounted policeman
patrols Princes Street
Right: coat of arms on the
entrance gate to Scone Palace

TIME DIFFERENCES

| GMT 12 noon | Scotland 12 noon | Germany 1PM | USA (NY) 7AM | Netherlands 1PM | Spain 1PM |

BEFORE YOU GO

WHAT YOU NEED

	Required	Suggested	Not required		UK	Germany	USA	Netherlands	Spain

● Required
○ Suggested
▲ Not required

Some countries require a passport to remain valid for a minimum period (usually at least six months) beyond the date of entry – contact their consulate or embassy or your travel agent for details.

	UK	Germany	USA	Netherlands	Spain
Passport	▲	●	●	●	●
Visa (regulations can change – check before booking your journey)	▲	▲	▲	▲	▲
Onward or Return Ticket	▲	○	○	○	○
Health Inoculations	▲	▲	▲	▲	▲
Health Documentation (➤ 123, Health)	▲	●	▲	●	●
Travel Insurance	○	○	○	○	○
Driving Licence (national)	●	●	●	●	●
Car Insurance Certificate (if own car)	▲	●	●	●	●
Car Registration Document (if own car)	▲	●	●	●	●

WHEN TO GO

Scotland

██ High season
▭ Low season

5°C	5°C	8°C	11°C	14°C	16°C	18°C	18°C	15°C	11°C	9°C	7°C
JAN	FEB	MAR	APR	MAY	JUN	JUL	AUG	SEP	OCT	NOV	DEC

🌧 Wet 🌤 Sun/ Showers

TOURIST OFFICES

In Scotland
Scottish Tourist Board
23 Ravelston Terrace,
Edinburgh EH4 3TP
☎ 0131 332 2433
fax: 0131 343 1513
Website:
www.visitscotland.com

In England
Scottish Tourist Board
19 Cockspur Street
London SW1 5BL
☎ 020 7930 2812
Fax: 020 7930 1817

In the USA
British Tourist Authority
551 Fifth Avenue,
Suite 701,
New York, NY 10176-0799
☎ 1 800 462 2748

POLICE 999

FIRE 999

AMBULANCE 999

WHEN YOU ARE THERE

ARRIVING

Scotland has four main international airports –
Glasgow, Edinburgh, Aberdeen and Prestwick.
Scheduled and charter flights arrive daily at all of
them from Europe, USA and the rest of the UK. There
are direct flights to Glasgow from North America.

Glasgow Airport	Journey times	
Kilometres to city centre	🚇	N/A
14 kilometres (9 miles)	🚌	20 minutes
	🚗	15 minutes

Edinburgh Airport	Journey times	
Kilometres to city centre	🚇	N/A
26 kilometres (16 miles)	🚌	20 minutes
	🚗	40 minutes

MONEY

The British unit of currency is the pound sterling,
divided into 100p (pence). Its symbol, placed before
the pounds is £. There are coins for 1 and 2p (copper),
5, 10, 20 and 50p (silver), £1 (gold-coloured), £2 (silver
and gold-coloured); and bank notes for 5, 10, 20, 50
and 100 pounds. Scotland, unlike the rest of the UK,
also has £1 banknotes. The pound is often referred to
as a quid i.e. £5 is five quid or a fiver, while £10 would
simply be called a tenner.

TIME

 Scottish time, like
the rest of the UK,
is on Greenwich
Mean Time. The clocks are
advanced by one hour in the
spring and brought back one
hour in the autumn.
Continental Europe is
always one hour ahead.

CUSTOMS

 YES

**Goods Obtained Duty Free
Outside the EU (Limits)**
Alcohol (over 22% vol): 1L
plus 2L still wine *or*
Alcohol (not over 22% vol): 2L
and 2L still table wine.
Cigarettes: 200 *or* Cigars: 50
or Tobacco: 250g
Perfume: 60cc, Toilet Water:
250cc.
Other goods: to the value of
£145
**Goods Obtained Duty and
Tax Paid inside the EU
(Guidance Limits)**
Alcohol (over 22% vol): 10L
Alcohol (not over 22% vol):
20L. Wine (max 60L
sparkling): 90L
Beer: 110L. Cigarettes: 3,200,
Cigars: 200, Cigarillos: 400,
Tobacco:3kg. Perfume and
Toilet Water: unlimited.
**You must be 17 or over to
benefit from the alcohol and
tobacco allowances.**

🚫 **NO**

Drugs, firearms, ammunition,
offensive weapons, obscene
materials, animals.

USA
09068 200290

Germany
0131-337 2323

Netherlands
0131-220 3226

Spain
0131-220 1843

WHEN YOU ARE THERE

TOURIST OFFICES

Edinburgh & Lothians
● 3 Princes Street (above
  Waverly Station)
  Edinburgh
  ☎ 0131 473 3800
  Fax: 0131 473 3881
  web site
  www.edinburgh.org

Greater Glasgow & Clyde Valley
● 11 George Square
  Glasgow
  ☎ 0141 204 4400
  Fax: 0141 221 3524

Aberdeen
● Exchange House
  26–28 Exchange Street
  Aberdeen
  ☎ 01224 288828
  Fax: 01224 288828

Dundee & Angus
● 21 Castle Street
  Dundee
  ☎ 01382 527527
  Fax: 01382 527550

Dumfries & Galloway
● 64 Whitesands
  Dumfries
  ☎ 01387 245550
  Fax: 01387 245551

Shetland
● Market Cross
  Lerwick
  Shetland
  ☎ 01595 693434
  Fax: 01595 695807

NATIONAL HOLIDAYS

J	F	M	A	M	J	J	A	S	O	N	D
2		(2)	(2)	2			1				2

Scottish public holidays may vary from place to place
and their dates from year to year, thus although the
capital Edinburgh may be on holiday at certain times,
other Scottish towns and cities will not necessarily
be having a public holiday. Major holidays are:

1 Jan	New Year's Day
2 Jan	Bank Holiday
Mar/Apr	Good Friday/Easter Monday
First Mon May	May Day Bank Holiday
Last Mon May	Spring Bank Holiday
Last Mon Aug	August Bank Holiday
25 Dec	Christmas Day
26 Dec	Boxing Day

OPENING HOURS

○ Shops	● Attractions/museums
● Offices	◐ Post offices
● Banks	◐ Pharmacies

9 AM	10 AM	11 AM	12 PM	1 PM	2 PM	3 PM	4 PM	5 PM	6 PM
	9:30	10:30	11:30	12:30	1:30	2:30	3:30	4:30	5:30

The above times are general and there are variations.
Shops will usually remain open throughout lunch and
even on Sundays in the larger towns, cities and
holiday resorts. Supermarkets will also be open
seven days and close between 7PM and 10PM but
several now offer 24-hour opening, mainly in the
cities. Markets are generally open 8–4.
In rural areas shops will close for an hour at lunch
time, generally 1–2PM, for one afternoon each week
and all day Sunday.

DRIVE ON THE LEFT

TOILETS CHARGE

★★ ★★

PUBLIC TRANSPORT

 Internal Flights
British Regional Airways (☎ 0345 222111) have scheduled flights linking the main cities and provide a regular service to the islands, including Orkney and Shetland.

 Trains
Most of Scotland's rail service is operated by Scotrail (☎ 0345 484950 – enquiries; 0345 550033 – bookings). GNER (☎ 0345 225225) and Virgin (☎ 0345 222333) also operate services on the main intercity routes and to the rest of the UK.

 Long Distance Buses
Scottish Citylink (☎ 0990 505050) covers most of the country as well as linking to the rest of the UK. The buses are mostly modern and comfortable. Several local companies provide linking services to areas not covered by Citylink and in the Highlands, Islands and remote rural areas there are Post Buses run by the Royal Mail (☎ 01463 256273).

 Ferries
Caledonian MacBrayne (☎ 0990 650000) has an extensive service covering the main island destinations on the West Coast including the Western Islands. For Orkney and Shetland, Northlink Ferries (☎ 01856 851144) have regular sailings from Aberdeen.

 Urban Transport
In the main towns and cities the public transport network is fairly extensive. Glasgow has Scotland's only underground and is also well served by urban trains and buses. Elsewhere a plethora of bus companies compete for passengers.

CAR RENTAL

 Most major companies have facilities at airports, major towns and cities. Advance booking can avoid lengthy waits at peak periods. Avis (☎ 0990 900500). Budget (☎ 0800 181181). Connect (☎ 08707 282828). Thrifty (☎ 0990 168238).

TAXIS

 In cities and larger towns the standard black hackney cabs are licensed, have meters and should display a tariff. Minicabs and private hire cars will also be licensed and may be metered. If not, agree a fare before entering the vehicle.

DRIVING

 Speed limit on motorways and dual carriageways **70mph**

 Speed limit on all other roads **60mph**

 Speed limits on urban roads **30mph**

 Seat belts must be worn in front and rear seats at all times.

 Breath testing: when involved in an accident or stopped by police for any reason. Limit: 30ml on breath/80mlgm in blood.

 Fuel (petrol) is expensive and available in two grades: Unleaded and Super Unleaded. Prices vary and it is considerably more expensive in the Highlands and Islands. The least expensive fuel can be found at supermarkets with filling stations. Opening hours are variable with some 24-hour stations on motorways and large urban areas.

 SOS telephones are located at regular intervals along motorways. A breakdown service operated by the Automobile Association (☎ 0800 887766) has a 24-hour breakdown service for members and for members of organisations with reciprocal agreements.

PERSONAL SAFETY

Theft from cars is unfortunately common, as is the usual crimes associated with big cities such as bag snatching and pickpockets. Any crime should be reported to the police and a report requested if an insurance claim is contemplated.

- Never leave anything of value in your car.
- Keep passports, tickets and valuables in a hotel safe deposit box.
- Don't keep valuables/ money in a bum bag. This signals tourist and is a magnet for pickpockets.
- Don't walk alone in dimly lit areas at night.

Police assistance
☎ **999** from any call box

TELEPHONES

Public telephones on the street and in bars, hotels and restaurants accept 10, 20, 50p, £1 and £2 coins, while others can only be used with phone cards (available from newsagents and post offices). Costs are considerably less expensive that using the phone in your hotel room.

International Dialling Codes	
From the UK to:	
France:	00 33
Germany:	00 49
Spain:	00 34
USA:	00 1
Netherlands:	00 31

POST

Each town and most large villages have at least one post office. Opening hours are 9–5:30 Mon–Fri and 9–12:30 Sat, closed Sun. Small offices close for lunch from 1–2PM. Stamps are also sold by some newsagents and shops selling postcards.

ELECTRICITY

The electricity supply is 240 volts. Sockets take square three pin plugs.

 All visitors from other countries will require an adaptor.

American appliances also require a voltage converter.

TIPS/GRATUITIES

Yes ✓   No ✗

Restaurants (if service not included)	✓	10%
Cafés/bars (only for meals)	✓	10%
Taxis	✓	10%
Porters	✓	£1/bag
Chambermaids	✓	£2
Hairdressers	✓	£1–2
Cloakroom attendants	✓	£1
Toilets	✗	
Theatre/cinema usherettes	✗	

What to photograph: picturesque villages, stunning coastline, magnificent castles perched on rocks and the spectacular scenery of the Highlands and islands.
Restrictions: anywhere that photography is not allowed will be clearly noted with warning signs.
Buying film: all popular brands, types of film and camera batteries are readily available and reasonably priced.

HEALTH

Insurance
Nationals of the EU and certain other countries receive free emergency medical treatment in the UK with the relevant documentation, although private medical insurance is still advised and is essential for all other visitors.

Dental Services
Dental treatment is very limited under the National Health Service scheme and even EU nationals will probably have to pay. However, private medical insurance will cover you.

Sun Advice
Strange as it seems in a country with a reputation for so much rain it is possible to get sunburn and sunstroke, particularly during the summer months. Avoid prolonged exposure and use sunblock or cover up.

Drugs
Prescription, non-prescription drugs and medicines are available from chemist shops. Non-prescription drugs and medicines are also widely available in supermarkets.

Safe Water
Tap water is generally safe to drink, particularly in rural areas and the Highlands.

CONCESSIONS

Students/Youths
Students will generally get a reduction in the entrance fees to museums and galleries on production of the International Student Identity Card (ISIC) or in some places their student matriculation card, provided it has a photo. The Young Person's Railcard gives a 33 per cent discount off all rail fares in the UK and the National Express Discount Card gives 30 per cent off coach fares.

Senior Citizens
Over 65s (men) and 60s (women) get a range of reductions in admissions to museums and galleries on proof of age. The Senior's Railcard provides a discount similar to the Young Person's and the National Express card is also available.

CLOTHING SIZES

USA	UK	Europe	
36	36	46	
38	38	48	
40	40	50	
42	42	52	Suits
44	44	54	
46	46	56	
8	7	41	
8.5	7.5	42	
9.5	8.5	43	
10.5	9.5	44	Shoes
11.5	10.5	45	
12	11	46	
14.5	14.5	37	
15	15	38	
15.5	15.5	39/40	
16	16	41	Shirts
16.5	16.5	42	
17	17	43	
6	8	34	
8	10	36	
10	12	38	
12	14	40	Dresses
14	16	42	
16	18	44	
6	4.5	38	
6.5	5	38	
7	5.5	39	
7.5	6	39	Shoes
8	6.5	40	
8.5	7	41	

WHEN DEPARTING

- Remember to reconfirm your homeward flight the day before departing.
- Check the duty-free limits of the country you are travelling to before departure.

LANGUAGE

The language of the country is English but even English-speaking people may have some difficulties with the Scots language when specifically Scots words are used. These will vary according to region. In Aberdeen the dialect is known as Doric, in the Lowlands of Scotland it is Lallans, the city of Glasgow has a patter all of its own and in Orkney and Shetland the local dialect has Scandinavian roots. Although you may not wish to use the dialects, knowing the most common dialect words will ease understanding.

Eating and drinking

ashet	a large serving dish
bannock	a round flat cake cooked on a girdle
brose	a type of porridge made from oats or pease-meal
bridie	a spicy meat and onion pasty
butterie or rowie	a croissant-like bread roll made with lots of butter
caller	fresh
tatties	potatoes
champit tatties	mashed potatoes
tattie scones	flat scone made of potatoes and flour cooked on a gridle
tattie bogle	scarecrow
clootie dumpling	a rich fruit cake boiled in a cloth to cook it
dram	a measure of whisky
drouth	thirst
drouthy	thirsty
gigot or shank	a leg of lamb or pork; gigot would normally be the thick end and shank the thin end
haggis	pudding made from offal, blood, oatmeal and spices, boiled in a sheep's stomach
messages	shopping, normally for groceries
piece	sandwich
play piece	playtime snack
jeelie piece	jam sandwich
piece break	mid-morning break
stovies	potatoes cooked with onion and a little meat
girdle	gridle or flat iron plate for cooking scones on top of the stove

General

aye	yes
naw	no
muckle	big
greet	to cry
greetin'-faced	a person who is always miserable
haiver	to talk rubbish

ken	to know
kenspeckle	well known
ceilidh	party or dance
speir	ask or enquire
stravaig	to wander abroad; being out on the town

People

bairn, chiel, wean	child
blether	to gossip
crabbit	bad-tempered
dour	sullen
hen, quine (NE), wifie, lassie	girl or woman
jimmy, loon (NE) laddie	man or boy
nyaff, scunner	an unpleasant person
peelie wallie	pale and ill looking
shilpit	thin
sleekit	sly
sonsie	healthy looking
thrawn	perverse

Geography and buildings

brae	hill
burn	a stream
cairn	a pile of stones used as a marker or memorial
furth	outside the area
glen	valley
kirk	church
sooth	south; in Orkney and Shetland refers to the mainland of Scotland

Weather

braw	good
dreich	grey and dull
droukit	soaked
glaur	mud
gloaming	evening
simmer dim	mid-summer when it never gets quite dark but the sun just dips below the horizon
smirr	just a little rain in the air
snell	cold
stoating	bouncing; used when describing heavy rain

INDEX

Abbotsford House 40
Aberdeen 75–76, 110–11
Aberdeen Fish Market and Harbour 75
Aberdeen Maritime Museum 75
accommodation 100–105
airports and air services 119, 121
Angus Glens 66
Anstruther 67
Arbigland 58
Arnol Black House 89
Arran 6, 12, 52
Auchindrain 69

Ballater 77
Balmaclellan 59
Balmoral 77
Balquhidder 73
banks 120
Bannockburn 72, 73
Barnaline 70
Barrie, J M 56, 69
bed and breakfast 100
Bettyhill 77
Biggar 43
Birkhill Clay Mine 66
Blair Drummond Safari Leisure Park 111
Bonawe Iron Furnace 70
Bo'ness and Kinniel Railway 66
Borders 40–43
Britannia 31
British Golf Museum 72
Brodick 52
Broughton House 57
Broughty Ferry and Castle 12, 63
Burns, Robert 14, 16, 56
Burns House Museum 56
Burns National Heritage Park 16
Burrell Collection 17
buses, long distance 121

Caerlaverock Castle and Wildfowl and Wetlands Trust Reserve 52–53
Cairngorms 7, 77
Caledonian Canal 80
Callanish Stones 13, 87, 89
Calton Hill 31
car rental 121
Carloway Broch 89
Castle Urquhart 83
Celtic music 6, 9, 113
Central Scotland 62–73
children's attractions 110–11
Chirnside 43
Clansmen's Centre 80
climate and seasons 7, 118
Coll 68
concessions 123
Connery, Sir Sean 14
consulates and high commissions 120
Crail 67

Crarae Garden 66
credit cards 103
Cromarty 80
Cruachan Power Station 70
Culloden Battlefield 18
Culross 67
Culzean Castle and Country Park 53
customs regulations 119

departure information 124
dialect words/phrases 124
discos, pubs and nightclubs 112–13
RRS *Discovery* 63
Dornoch 80
drinking water 123
drives
    Central Scotland 65
    Edinburgh and the Borders 43
    Harris and Lewis 89
    Southwest Scotland 59
driving 118, 121
drugs and medicines 123
Dumfries 56
Dunaskin Open Air Museum 56
Dundee 63–64, 111
Dunkeld 13
Duns 43
Dunstaffanage Castle 71
Dynamic Earth 110

East Neuk of Fife 65, 67
eating out 38–39, 92–99
Edinburgh 12, 30–37, 43, 110
Edinburgh Castle 9, 19
electricity 122
emergency telephone numbers 119
entertainment 112–16

Falls of Measach 90
The Falkirk Wheel Experience 67
ferry services 121
festivals and events 9, 111, 116
Floors Castle 41
food and drink 9, 60–61
    see also eating out
Fort George 81
Fort William 81
Foula 84

Gallery of Modern Art 48
Galloway Forest Park and Glentrool 56
geography 7
Glasgow 9, 12, 17, 25, 44–51
Glasgow Harbour 50
Glasgow School of Art 48
Glen Affric 81
Glen Clova 66
Glen Coe 20–21
Glenkiln Reservoir 59
Glenlee 50
Grassmarket 32, 107
Great Glen 80

Haddington 40
Harris 89
health 118, 123
Helensburgh 68
Highland Clearances 11, 74, 77
Highland Folk Museum 82
Highlands 74–83
Hill House 68
history of Scotland 10–11
Holmwood House 49
hostels 104

Inner Hebrides 68
insurance 118, 123
Inveraray 69
Inverewe Gardens 82
Inverness 82
Iona 68
Islay 68
Italian Chapel 85

James Patterson Museum 59
Jarlshof 84
Jedburgh 41
John Paul Jones birthplace museum 58, 59
Jura 68

Kellie Castle 67
Kelso 41
Kelvingrove Art Gallery and Museum 49
Kilchurn Castle 70
Kingussie 82–83
Kirkcudbright 57
Kirkwall 85
Kirriemuir 69
Lairig Ghru 77
Leckmelm Shrubbery and Arboretum 90
Lennoxlove 40
Lerwick 85
Lewis 87–88, 89
Lewis Loom Centre 88
Linlithgow 69, 111
local knowledge 38–39
Loch Awe 70
Loch Katrine 73
Loch Leven Castle 65
Loch Lomond 70
Loch Ness 83
Loch Tummel 8
Lower Largo 65

Machars 57
Mackintosh, Charles Rennie 48, 50, 51, 68
McManus Art Gallery and Museum 64
Maes Howe 85
maps
    Edinburgh 34–35
    Glasgow 46–47
    Northern Scotland 78–79
    Scotland 28–29
    Southern Scotland 54–55
Mary, Queen of Scots 10, 11, 14, 19, 65, 69

measurements/sizes 122, 123
medical and dental treatment 123
Mellerstain House 41
Melrose 9, 41, 111
Mills Observatory 64
money 119
Moniaive 59
Montrose Basin Wildlife Centre 70
Mousa Broch/Island 86
Mull 68
Museum of Scotland 9, 32
Museum of Transport 49

national holidays 120
New Abbey 58
New Lanark 22
Northern Scotland 74–90

Oban 71
Ocean Frontier, Fort William 81
Official Loch Ness Exhibition Centre 83
opening hours 120
Orkney 13, 24, 84, 85

Palace of Holyroodhouse 33
Palnackie 59
Pass of Killiecrankie 72
passports and visas 118
People's Story 33
personal safety 122
Perth 71
pharmacies 120, 123
photography 123
Pitlochry 72
Pittenweem 65, 67
police 119, 122

population 7
postal services 120, 122
Princes Street 33
Princes Street Gardens 36
Provost Skene's House 76
public transport 121

Raasay Outdoor Centre 88
Regimental Museum of the Queen's Own Highlanders 81
Robert the Bruce 10, 45
Robert Smail's Printing Works 42
Rosslyn Chapel 13, 23
Rothiemurchus 83

St Abbs 42, 43
St Andrews 72
St Magnus Cathedral 85
Samye Ling Tibetan Centre 58
Satrosphere Science Centre 76
Scone Palace 71
Scotland Street School Museum 50
Scott, Sir Walter 40
Scottish Fisheries Museum 67
Scottish National Portrait Gallery 36, 37
Scottish Parliament 7, 11, 36, 38
Secret Bunker 65
senior citizens 123
Shetland 84–5
shopping 106–9, 120
Skara Brae 24
Skye 87, 88, 111
Skye Museum of Island Life 88
Southwest Scotland 45, 52–59
sports and leisure 39, 115
Stirling 62, 72–73, 111

Strathnaver Museum 77
students/young travellers 123
Summer Isles 90
sun advice 123
Sweetheart Abbey 58

tartan 38, 106
taxis 121
telephones 122
Tenement House, Glasgow 25
theatres 114
time differences 118, 119
tipping 122
Tiree 68
toilets 121
Tolbooth Museum 76
tourist offices 118, 120
trains 121
Traquair House 26
Trimontium Exhibition 41
Trossachs 73

Ullapool 90
Unicorn 63
Up Helly Aa 85

Verdant Works 64

walks
  Edinburgh 37
  Glasgow 51
  Mousa Island 86
Wallace, William 10, 14, 45
Wallace Monument 73
Waverley paddle steamer 38, 53
Western Isles 87–90
whisky 9, 61, 68, 109
Whithorn 57
Wigtown 57
Willow Tea Rooms 51

Acknowledgements

The Automobile Association wishes to thank the following photographers, libraries and associations for their assistance in the preparation of this book:

BRIDGEMAN ART LIBRARY, LONDON 17b The Rehearsal, c1877 by Edgar Degas (1834–1917), Burrell Collection, Glasgow, Scotland, 37b Prince Charles Edward Stewart alias 'Bonnie Prince Charlie' (1720–88), 1732, (oil on canvas) by Antonio David (1702–66), Scottish National Portrait Gallery, Scotland; MARY EVANS PICTURE LIBRARY 10,11a,14b; McMANUS GALLERIES 64b; MRI BANKERS' GUIDE TO FOREIGN CURRENCY 119; Parliament Copyright. The Scottish Parliament Corporate Body 1999, 11c; SPECTRUM COLOUR LIBRARY 9c, 18b, 86b; HUGH TAYLOR 23b, 24b, 26b, 32, 50b, 85. The remaining photographs are from the Association's own library (AA PHOTO LIBRARY) and with contributions from M Adelman 52b; M Alexander 9b, 87b; Adrian Baker 1, 2, 77b; Jeff Beazley 13a, 27a, 40, 53b, 57b, 58b, 66, P & G Bowater 72b; Jim Carnie 6c, 7b, 27b, 67b, 70b, 117b; Douglas Corrance 28, 29, 30, 34, 35, 37a, 42a, 43a; Steve Day 6b, 8b, 13b, 38, 39, 64, 64a, 65a, 65b, 68a, 71a, 72a, 73a, 91b; Eric Ellington 60b, 75b, 76b, 84b, 90b, 122a; Richard Elliot 15b, 68b, 89b; Derek Forss 42b; Stephen Gibson 15a, 16a, 17a, 18a, 19a, 20a, 21a, 22a, 22b, 23a, 24a, 25a, 25b, 26a, 44, 45, 46, 47, 48a, 48b, 49, 50a, 51a, 52a, 53a, 54, 55, 57a, 58a, 59a, 60a, 61a; Jim Henderson 5a, 6a, 7a, 8a, 9a, 11b, 12a, 14a, 20/21, 61b, 81, 88; Cameron Lees 5b; Rich Newton 51b; Ken Paterson 12b, 31b, 33b, 63b, 69b, 74a, 75a, 76a, 77a, 78, 79, 82a, 84a, 86a, 87a, 89a, 90a, 91a, 92, 93, 94, 95, 96, 97, 98, 99, 100, 101, 102, 103, 104, 105, 106, 107, 108, 109, 110, 111, 112, 113, 114, 115, 116, 117a, 122b, 122c; Peter Sharp 16b, 41b, 56b, 80; Michael Taylor 19b, 83; Ronnie Weir 21b, 73b

Author's Acknowledgements

Hugh Taylor and Moira McCrossan would like to thank Mike Blair, Calmac; John Yellowlees, Scotrail; Andy Naylor, GNER; Alan McLean, Virgin; Moira Dyer, Glasgow and Clyde Valley Tourist Board and Maurice Mullay, Shetland Tourist Board for their help.

Revision management: Pam Stagg Page layout: Jo Tapper

The Atlas

Photo Montage	130–31
Useful Websites	132
Atlas Symbols	133
Atlas	134–44

Acknowledgements

All pictures are from AA World Travel Library with contributions from the following photographers:
Steve Day: Highland cattle, steam train pulling out of Glenfinnan Station
Ken Paterson: Princes Street from Calton Hill, Grassmarket cafés
Jonathan Smith: Edinburgh Military Tattoo

The Automobile Association
www.theAA.com
Comprehensive and up-to-the-minute information covering AA-approved hotels, guest houses and B&Bs, restaurants and pubs, along with the latest traffic information and detailed routes to your destination in the UK. Also online access to breakdown cover, insurance, the AA Driving School and Bookshop and much more.

Scottish Tourist Board
www.visitscotland.com

Edinburgh & Lothians Tourist Board
www.edinburgh.org

National Trust for Scotland
www.nts.org

Southern Upland Way
www.dumgal.gov.uk/southernuplandway

Speyside Way
www.speysideway.org

West Highland Way
www.westhighlandway.com

GENERAL

City of Edinburgh Museums and Galleries
www.cac.org.uk

Edinburgh Fringe Festival
www.edfringe.com

Edinburgh Hogmanay
www.edinburghhogmanay.org

Glasgow International Jazz Festival
www.jazzfest.co.uk

Great Glen Way
www.greatglenway.com

Historic Scotland
www.historic-scotland.gov.uk

International Arts Festival
www.eif.co.uk

The Isle of Skye, Lochalsh & Raasay
www.skye.co.uk

Military Tattoo
www.edintattoo.co.uk

National Gallery of Scotland
www.nationalgalleries.org

National Museums of Scotland
www.nms.ac.uk

Royal Highland Show
www.rhass.org.uk

TRAVEL

Flights and Information
www.cheapflights.co.uk
www.thisistravel.co.uk
www.ba.com
www.worldairportguide.com

Caledonian MacBrayne
www.calmac.co.uk

Citylink
www.citylink.co.uk

John o'Groats Ferries Ltd
www.jogferry.co.uk

National Express
www.nationalexpress.com

National Rail Enquiry Service
www.nationalrail.co.uk

Public Transport Timetable Enquiries
www.travelinescotland.com

Royal Mail Postbus
www.postbus.royalmail.com

Scotrail
www.scotrail.co.uk

Seacat Scotland
www.seacat.co.uk

Stena Line
www.stenaline.co.uk

Motorway / Autobahn / Autoroute / Autopista / Autostrada

National road, dual carriageway / Zweibhnige Nationalstrasse /
Route nationale à chaussées séparées / Carretera nacional de doble vía /
Strada nazionale a doppia carreggiata

National road, single carriageway / Einbahnige Nationalstrasse /
Route nationale à chaussées unique / Carretera nacional de vía unica /
Strada nazionale a singola carreggiata

Other main road / Haupistrasse / Autre route de liaison principale /
Otra carretera principal / Strada di grande comunicazione

M20
A2
Road numbering: Motorway, other road / Strassennumerierung:
Autobahn, Sonstige Strasse / Numérotation: Autoroute,
Autre route / Numeración de las carreteras: Autopista, Otra carretera /
Numero di strada: Autostrada, Altra strada

Junction / Anschlussstelle / Échangeur / Acceso / Svincolo

Restricted junction / Beschränkte Anschlußstelle / Échangeur partiel /
Acceso parcial / Svincolo con limitazione

Service area / Tankstelle / Aire de service / Área de servicio /
Area di servizio

Internal boundary / Verwaltungsgrenze / Frontière intérieure /
Límite interno / Confine interno

GLASGOW ✈ International airport / Internationaler Flughafen / Aéroport international /
Aeropuerto internacional / Aeroporto internazionale

National park / Nationalpark / Parc national / Parque nacional /
Parco nazionale

```
0                                              50 km
|————————————————|————————————————|
0                                              30 miles
```

Maps © Mairs Geographischer Verlag / Falk Verlag, 73751 Ostfildern

Gallan Head

Ste
(S

A858

WESTERN IS

Scarp

A859

Taransay

Tairbeart
(Tarbert)

*Toe
Head*

Harris

Pabbay

Sound of Harris

Uibhist a Tuath
(North Uist)

Loch nam Madadh
(Lochmaddy)

A867

The Little Minch

Beinn na Faoghla
(Benbecula)

Dunvegan

A865

Uibhist a Deas
(South Uist)

Isle
of
Sky

Loch Baghasdail
(Lochboisdale)

Eriskay

Sound of Barra

Canna

Barraigh
(Barra)

A888

Bagh a Chaisteil
(Castlebay)

O u t e r   H e b r i d e s

I

Shetland
Islands

Unst

A968

Yell

Fetlar

A970

2

A968

Whalsay

Mainland

A971

SHETLAND
ISLANDS

Scalloway

Lerwick

Foula

A970

3

North
Ronaldsay

Westray

Sanday

4

Orkney
Islands

Rousay

Stronsay

A966

Mainland

Shapinsay

Stromness

A965

Kirkwall

A964

ORKNEY
ISLANDS

A960

Hoy

South
Ronaldsay

5

Island of
Stroma

Scrabster

John o'Groats

A836

A9

A99

HIGHLAND